FEMINIST PERSPECTIVES ON BIBLICAL SCHOLARSHIP

SOCIETY OF BIBLICAL LITERATURE
BIBLICAL SCHOLARSHIP IN NORTH AMERICA

Kent Harold Richards, Editor

ADELA YARBRO COLLINS,
Editor

FEMINIST PERSPECTIVES
ON BIBLICAL SCHOLARSHIP

Scholars Press
Atlanta, Georgia

SOCIETY OF BIBLICAL LITERATURE
CENTENNIAL PUBLICATIONS

Editorial Board

The Society of Biblical Literature gratefully acknowledges a grant from the National Endowment for the Humanities to underwrite certain editorial and research expenses of the Centennial Publications Series. Published results and interpretations do not necessarily represent the view of the Endowment.

Library of Congress Cataloging in Publication Data
Main entry under title:

Feminist perspectives on biblical scholarship.

(Biblical scholarship in North America ; no. 10)
(Centennial publications / Society of Biblical Literature)
Bibliography: p.
1. Bible—Criticism, interpretation, etc.—North
America—History—19th century—Addresses, essays, lectures.
2. Bible—Criticism, interpretation, etc.—North
America—History—20th century—Addresses, essays, lectures.
3. Feminism—Religious aspects—Addresses, essays, lectures.
4. Women in the Bible—Addresses, essays, lectures. 5. Society of
Biblical Literature—History—Addresses, essays, lectures. I. Collins,
Adela Yarbro. II. Title. III. Series. IV. Series: Centennial
publications (Society of Biblical Literature)
BS500.F43   1984   220.6'088042   84-13947
ISBN 0-89130-774-5
ISBN 0-89130-773-7 (pbk.)

Printed in the United States of America
on acid-free paper

CONTENTS

Editor and Contributors

BERNADETTE J. BROOTEN is Project Director within the "Frau und Christentum" project of the Institut für ökumenische Forschung, University of Tübingen, Assistant Professor of Religion at the Claremont Graduate School, and Director of Research in Women's Studies, Institute for Antiquity and Christianity, Claremont, California. She is at present working on a study of Romans 1:26 within the context of Paul's understanding of female and male and within the context of discussions of lesbian existence in the Greco-Roman world.

ADELA YARBRO COLLINS is Professor in New Testament at McCormick Theological Seminary. She is the author of *The Combat Myth in the Book of Revelation, The Apocalypse,* and *Crisis and Catharsis: The Power of the Apocalypse.*

ELISABETH SCHÜSSLER FIORENZA is Professor of Theology at Notre Dame University. She is the author of *Priester für Gott, Invitation to the Book of Revelation,* and *In Memory of Her: A Feminist Theological Reconstruction of Christian Origins.*

ESTHER FUCHS is Assistant Professor of Hebrew Literature at the Department of Oriental and African Languages and Literatures at the University of Texas at Austin. She is the author of *Encounters With Israeli Authors* and *No License to Die.* Her work *Cunning Innocence: An Introduction to the Ironic Art of S.Y. Agnon* is in press. She is currently working on a book entitled *Sexual Politics in the Biblical Narrative.*

NELLY FURMAN is Associate Professor in the Department of Romance Studies at Cornell University, where she teaches nineteenth-century French literature and French feminist theories. She organized the literary section of the book *Women and Language in Literature and Society,* edited by Sally McConnell-Ginet, Ruth Borker, and Nelly Furman.

CAROLYN DE SWARTE GIFFORD is the Coordinator of the Women's History Project of the General Commission on Archives and History of the United Methodist Church. She received her doctorate in History and Literature of Religions from Northwestern University. She has contributed articles to volumes on both women and religion in America and the history of spirituality.

CAROLYN OSIEK is Associate Professor of New Testament at Catholic Theological Union in Chicago, with a doctorate in New Testament and Christian Origins from Harvard University. She teaches and has written several articles on the role of women in New Testament and Early Christianity. She is the author of *Rich and Poor in the Shepherd of Hermas: An Exegetical-Social Investigation.*

T. DRORAH SETEL is a student at the Harvard Divinity School. She wrote and presented "A Jewish-Feminist Response to Elisabeth Schüssler Fiorenza's 'Toward a Feminist Biblical Hermeneutics: Biblical Interpretation and Liberation Theology'" at the session of the Feminist Hermeneutic Project at the Annual Meeting of the AAR and SBL in New York in 1982. She responded to a paper by Marla Selvidge on Mark 5:24–35 at the session on Women in the Biblical World at the same meeting. U

INTRODUCTION

Adela Yarbro Collins

To introduce this volume, I would like to do three things. First is briefly to sketch the way in which this volume came into being. Its origin clarifies its purpose and the needs it is intended to address. Second comes a description of how the volume was conceived and why the particular topics of these essays were selected. Finally, I will suggest what the essays have achieved and indicate areas where further work is needed.

The Context

In 1980 the Society of Biblical Literature celebrated its centennial. Several years prior to that date, a Centennial Publications Program was initiated to mark the event. This program was to be guided by a Centennial Editorial Committee.

The program for the Annual Meeting in 1980 departed from the usual pattern to provide an opportunity to reflect upon the SBL's history and prospects for the future. One session was devoted to women and the Bible under the general rubric "The History and Sociology of Biblical Scholarship." A number of women scholars, coordinated by Phyllis Trible of Union Theological Seminary in New York, organized a panel to explore "The Effects of Women's Studies on Biblical Studies."[1] This session was the first program unit of any SBL Annual Meeting to be devoted specifically to women. The existence of this session only made more apparent that women are a minority in the SBL and that feminism has made little impact on the guild.

As plans for the Centennial Publications Program became public, it was pointed out that women were not represented on the Centennial Publications Editoral Committee and that the projected publications virtually ignored the experience of women, feminist exegesis, and feminist hermeneutics. My election to the Centennial Publications Editorial Committee in December 1980 resulted from an effort on the part of the committee to ensure at least that women would have a representative in the

---

[1] The members of the panel were Mary Wakeman, Kathy Sakenfeld, Elisabeth Schüssler Fiorenza, Adela Yarbro Collins, Letty Russell, and Rosemary Radford Ruether. The presentations of the panelists have been published with an introduction by Phyllis Trible in the *Journal for the Study of the Old Testament* 22 (1982).

remainder of the planning process and in the editorial work itself.

At the first meeting of the committee which I attended, 31 January to 1 February 1981, six types of Centennial Publications were consolidated into four series: Biblical Scholarship in North America, The Bible and Its Modern Interpreters, Biblical Scholarship in Confessional Perspective, and The Bible in American Culture. Biblical Scholarship in North America was to have two sub-series: Monographs on Scholars and Monographs on Disciplines and Schools. At that time a few volumes had appeared and many were assigned. As far as we could determine at that point, the only place in which the experience of women as women was to be the subject of study in the projected publications was in one of the volumes in the series The Bible in American Culture: *The Bible and Social Reform*, edited by Ernest Sandeen (Chico, CA: Scholars Press, 1982). Barbara Brown Zikmund, of the Pacific School of Religion in Berkeley, California, has an essay in the volume entitled "Biblical Arguments and Women's Place in the Church."

A consensus rapidly developed that we needed a volume that would focus on feminist exegesis and hermeneutics. Shortly after that meeting I made a proposal in writing to the other members of the committee for a volume entitled *Feminist Perspectives on Biblical Scholarship*. The proposal was accepted and the projected volume listed as part of the sub-series, Monographs on Disciplines and Schools, of the series Biblical Scholarship in North America.

At the Annual Meeting of the SBL in 1981, a consultation was held on "Women in the Biblical World," organized by Catherine Clark Kroeger of St. Paul, Minnesota. At the 1982 Annual Meeting, the consultation was chaired by Catherine Kroeger and Bernadette Brooten. Included was a panel of women biblical scholars discussing their work. As a member of that panel, I was given the opportunity to describe this projected book. Mary Ann Tolbert of Vanderbilt University was also on the panel. She spoke about an issue of *Semeia*, the SBL's experimental journal for biblical criticism, which she was editing on the Bible and feminist hermeneutics. The response to both our projects was very encouraging. Four essays came to be in this book because of conversations begun at that session.[2] In 1983 "Women in the Biblical World" became one of the regular sections in the program of the SBL Annual Meeting.

The Plan

In proposing and planning the volume, my intention was to explore the tension between historical-critical scholarship and feminism. In her

---

[2] I would like to thank Miri Amihai of Cornell University for putting me in contact with Nelly Furman and Esther Fuchs. Drorah Setel responded to a paper presented prior to the panel. The volume edited by Mary Ann Tolbert has appeared: *Semeia* 28 (1983).

presentation on the panel "The Effects of Women's Studies on Biblical Studies" at the Annual Meeting in 1980, Dorothy Bass showed that the development of a feminist hermeneutic and the rise of women biblical scholars were two quite separate processes from the late nineteenth century through at least the first half of the twentieth century.[3] A telling illustration of the gap between the two movements is Elizabeth Cady Stanton's explanation of the refusal of women biblical scholars to participate in *The Woman's Bible* project (1895–1898). She said that they declined "afraid that their high reputation and scholarly attainments might be compromised by taking part in an enterprise that for a time may prove very unpopular."[4]

Stanton's explanation is certainly plausible. One may ask, however, whether there were deeper reasons as well. Dorothy Bass and Carolyn De Swarte Gifford, in her essay in this volume, have pointed out the similarities between nineteenth-century feminist interpretation of the Bible and historical-critical scholarship. Both challenged the doctrines of the inerrancy of scripture and of an absolute, timeless revelation. But there were significant differences as well. Perhaps the most striking is the value placed by historical critics on objectivity, a value that contrasts with the feminists' commitment to interpreting the Bible in the service of the movement toward social reform with regard to the role of women. Few historical critics today would claim to be absolutely objective or totally value-free. The impossibility of experiencing another epoch as people living then experienced it and the difficulty even of becoming aware of our own presuppositions, let alone compensating for them or removing them, are widely recognized. Nevertheless, the standards of the guild still place a high value on understanding a text in terms of its original context or its objective character as text. The interpreter is expected to put aside her own convictions and desires, at least at the stage of exegesis in which the author's intention or the meaning(s) of the text is determined. At all stages of the process, the interpreter is expected to be self-critical.

Thus, the women biblical scholars invited by Elizabeth Cady Stanton to work on *The Woman's Bible* may have declined because they had been socialized to value objectivity more than commitment. The tension between the two virtues is acutely felt by many biblical scholars today, women and men. The same tension exists for ministers and lay people who are aware of historical criticism and wish to be responsible interpreters and who are also desirous of social change.

---

[3] Dorothy C. Bass, "Women's Studies and Biblical Studies: An Historical Perspective," *Journal for the Study of the Old Testament* 22 (1982) 6–12.

[4] Quoted by Dorothy Bass, "Women's Studies," 11.

In the past, women biblical scholars were active in reform movements but did biblical studies in the traditional manner.[5] Today, many of us are writing feminist exegesis and hermeneutics. In many cases, however, we have two separate audiences. We write articles and books for the guild which do not raise feminist issues and feminist articles and books for the women's movement. This compartmentalization is ambiguous. It could mean that no exegesis is neutral or absolutely valid and that the results depend on the context. It may be that the compartmentalization is only apparent and that the insights gained in each type of work affect the other. A few women seem fully to have integrated their scholarship and their feminism. This integration is more common among women who have recently completed their degrees. It remains to be seen what effect they will have on the guild.

There are many types of feminist exegesis and hermeneutics. Carolyn De Swarte Gifford shows that the first type to appear in the nineteenth century was feminist proof-texting. In their struggle for empowerment, nineteenth-century women discovered passages supportive of women which they could use to counter the biblical passages quoted by those who wished to keep women "in their place." In some cases the practice of proof-texting led to theological reflection on why certain texts were chosen and to the articulation of a hermeneutical principle, such as Jesus being women's emancipator. Another type of feminist interpretation that was practiced in the nineteenth century was the study and lifting up of historical women or female literary characters in the Bible, such as Deborah, Ruth, or Judith, as role models for women. Toward the end of the nineteenth century, under the leadership of Elizabeth Cady Stanton, feminist critical assessment of the biblical texts themselves as sexist was begun. Taken together these approaches could be called the first stage of feminist hermeneutics. All are still in use today.

In the twentieth century, more complex and sophisticated types of feminist hermeneutics have developed. In circles where proof-texting is regarded as a naïve use of the Bible but where biblical authority plays a predominant role, further work has been done in articulating critical hermeneutical principles that are based on aspects of the Bible itself. Letty Russell's articulation of salvation as liberation and blessing (*shalom*) is an example of this type.[6] Rosemary Radford Ruether has argued for the presence of a critical prophetic principle in the Bible which can be used as a criterion in interpreting particular texts.[7]

---

[5] Ibid., 10.

[6] Letty Russell, *Human Liberation in a Feminist Perspective—A Theology* (Philadelphia: Westminster, 1974) 104–13.

[7] Rosemary Radford Ruether, "Feminism and Patriarchal Religion: Principles of Ideological Critique of the Bible," *Journal for the Study of the Old Testament* 22 (1982) 54–66.

It is now widely recognized that the women who appear in biblical texts cannot function unambiguously as role models for women seeking empowerment today. The reason is that, whether historical persons or literary characters, these women are enmeshed in patriarchy and are presented and behave in androcentric ways. Their stories are still powerful, however, as Phyllis Trible has amply demonstrated. She has analyzed such narratives to show how the stories of ancient and modern women living in patriarchal culture intersect.[8]

Elisabeth Schüssler Fiorenza has accepted Elizabeth Cady Stanton's judgment that the Bible is thoroughly androcentric. Unlike some other feminists of the twentieth century who have reached that conclusion, she does not think it should therefore be left behind. Her proposal involves a threefold approach to the Bible. Its sexist characteristics should be pointed out and rejected as being unauthoritative. By using the methods developed by feminist historians writing women's history, women should be written back into the biblical texts where they are now virtually invisible. Ways in which the Bible has empowered women should be lifted up and proclaimed.[9]

These approaches developed in the twentieth century may be seen as a second stage of feminist hermeneutics. This volume was planned to do at least two things: to explore the tension between historical criticism and feminism and to contribute to the development of the methods and to the achieving of the goals of the second stage of feminist hermeneutics.

The original plan for the volume involved an introduction, followed by a historical essay, which would provide a historical perspective on the issues. Three methodological essays were planned. One was to treat problems in translating Hebrew, Aramaic, and Greek, the issue of inclusive language, and how the two intersect. Another was to focus on exegetical method, discussing the possibility of objective and value-free scholarship and raising the question whether historical-critical scholarship is inherently androcentric (male-centered) or even sexist (oppressive of women). The third was to treat historical methods, especially attempts to discern the relative social status of women and men in the regions and times related to the interpretation of biblical texts. The final section was to consist of several essays that would exemplify feminist exegesis or hermeneutics by interpreting particular texts.

---

[8] Phyllis Trible, *God and the Rhetoric of Sexuality* (Philadelphia: Fortress, 1978); see now also her *Texts of Terror: Literary-Feminist Readings of Biblical Narratives* (Philadelphia: Fortress, 1984).

[9] Elisabeth Schüssler Fiorenza, *In Memory of Her: A Feminist Theological Reconstruction of Christian Origins* (New York: Crossroad, 1983).

Results and Prospects

The original plan was modified as contributions were invited and conversations began about the project. The essay on translation and inclusive language was not ready in time to be included. I hope that it will be published elsewhere in the near future. Two methodological essays were added, Carolyn Osiek's analysis of feminist hermeneutical alternatives, including an assessment of the strengths and weaknesses of each, and Drorah Setel's essay on feminist methodology.

Historical perspective is crucial in reflecting on the tension between historical criticism and feminism and in discerning the prospects for feminist interpretation. It is also appropriate to trace the history of the interaction between or parallel development of critical biblical studies and the women's movement, given that this volume is part of the Centennial Publications Program of the SBL. With these considerations in mind, Carolyn De Swarte Gifford agreed to do the historical essay in this volume, "American Women and the Bible: The Nature of Woman as a Hermeneutical Issue." Her essay reconstructs for us a part of our heritage. She reminds us how our foresisters came to a critical feminist consciousness, how they explored the issues and struggled to change society. As we compare the hermeneutical methods of twentieth-century feminists with those of the nineteenth century, we can celebrate the progress in developing appropriate and adequate methods. At the same time, we are reminded—if we needed reminding—that for much of North American society, the issues and presuppositions have not changed. Many are those who still hold to the notion that the Bible contains timeless revelation about the role of women and that our role is one of subordination. Much work remains to be done in education and political action for social change.

Drorah Setel's essay, "Feminist Insights and the Question of Method," examines some of the fundamental presuppositions of Western academic inquiry and assesses them in terms of feminism as a distinctive world view. She challenges the notion of objectivity because it leads to the separation of inquirer and inquiry and is related to a dualistic philosophical framework, a framework that is inseparable from oppression. In the place of this objective dualistic framework, a world view which sees significance in connection and relationship is called for. She gives some very suggestive indications of the kinds of changes in our theoretical frameworks and terminology such a shift in world view would require. Many would argue that this shift is necessary to achieve justice for women and other non-elite groups. Some would argue, such as Owen Barfield, that it is needed if the human race is to survive at all.

Elisabeth Schüssler Fiorenza's essay, "Remembering the Past in Creating the Future: Historical-Critical Scholarship and Feminist Biblical

Interpretation," begins with the issue of exegetical method. She explores the tension between historical criticism and feminist interpretation in terms of their different views of the nature and purpose of history and historical research. She argues that the tension is due primarily to the fact that many historical critics are operating with a view of history that philosophers of history have left behind. The notion of objectivity has given way to a sense of radical historical conditioning and relativity. The value of disinterest has been replaced by the recognition that history is always history for a certain purpose and a certain group. Feminist interpreters are conscious of and explicit about their purposes and audience. Most historical critics need to become more self-conscious and outspoken in these regards.

In her essay, "Early Christian Women and Their Cultural Context: Issues of Method in Historical Reconstruction," Bernadette Brooten assesses the way in which early Christian women and their counterparts of other faiths have been studied. From the perspective of insights gained from women's historians and on the basis of other considerations, the current scholarly framework and methods are judged to be inappropriate and misleading. For the most part, women are not studied; rather, the focus is on what men thought about women. The latter is a legitimate subject of study, but it is not women's history. Because of the scarcity of evidence about women's lives, reconstructing the history of women in the biblical period is comparable to writing the history of both women and men in prehistorical time. The task is not impossible, but difficult. The results are bound to be tentative. These facts should not be discouraging, however, when we reflect on the partial character of the histories already written, which make not only women but also non-elite men invisible. We need to reevaluate our notions of history and what count as significant questions and data. Ms. Brooten makes creative and persuasive suggestions about how the study of early Christian women should be restructured: a new perspective, new questions, and a new framework are required. New sources, that is, extant data that are virtually ignored, must be taken into account.

Carolyn Osiek, in her essay "The Feminist and the Bible: Hermeneutical Alternatives," places the hermeneutical discussion in context by outlining the current situation with regard to feminism and biblical interpretation. Following Rosemary Radford Ruether, she discerns four major directions in contemporary feminism: liberal, social/Marxist, romantic/radical, and liberation-hermeneutical. With regard to biblical interpretation, she notes that the historical-critical method can no longer claim to be *the* method. Its limits and prejudices have been recognized and its use is being complemented by a variety of other methods. Her own articulation of the hermeneutical alternatives involves five types: rejectionist, loyalist, revisionist, sublimationist, and liberationist. Ms. Osiek herself views these as genuine alternatives, the choice among them being influenced by our conditioning and experience.

The following are my own reflections on the alternatives as she has delineated them. It would seem that a rapprochement between any one of these approaches and historical-critical methods is possible. Attempts have certainly been made, some more, some less successful. For those of us who value both the Bible and feminism, the rejectionist stance is not appealing. It is difficult to be a Christian and judge that the Bible is not authoritative or useful. Abandoning the Bible would greatly reduce women's sense that we have a heritage, and as Judy Chicago has said, "Our heritage is our power." Such a stance would also put considerable strain on the solidarity between women who have rejected the Bible and those who have not. The loyalist approach is problematic for the opposite reason. In this mode of interpreting and being, Christian commitment is natural and unproblematic, but it is difficult or even impossible to integrate into it the more profound insights and urgent calls for social change which have originated among feminists.

The other three alternatives seem more promising as means of integrating Christian faith and feminism. The choice among them is related to one's understanding of feminism, one's politics, and one's sense of how Christian faith relates to both. The revisionist approach is based on liberal values and works to minimize the difference between men and women. The sublimationist approach, on the other hand, assumes that there are deep-rooted and wide-ranging differences between men and women beyond the biological and that there are "masculine" and "feminine" qualities. As Drorah Setel points out, such language may reflect (socially contructed) reality, but it is not true. It may be useful in analyzing our current cultural situation but is of limited value in transforming the roles of women and men in our society. The liberationist approach is related to a vision of a whole new society. It calls not only for restructuring of the relations between women and men but also for a redistribution of wealth and a reorganization of social structures as a whole. It is the most ambitious and challenging of the approaches.

The essays by Nelly Furman and Esther Fuchs are examples of feminist hermeneutics which deal with particular texts. In her essay, "His Story versus Her Story: Male Genealogy and Female Strategy in the Jacob Cycle," Nelly Furman offers an interpretation of the Jacob cycle which draws upon semiotics, audience criticism, deconstruction, and feminism. The result is both striking and intriguing. She shows that in this cycle garments have both "his story" and "her story" to tell. For the male characters, garments have a fixed meaning that establishes special relationships among men, a channel of communication from which women are excluded. For the female characters, garments are signifiers open to a variety of meanings. The female characters use garments to insert themselves into the communicative process. The distinctive ways in which male and female characters use garments in the narratives become in Ms. Furman's hands a metaphor for two types of interpretation, an androcentric and a feminist, neither of which can claim to be neutral.

In her essay "The Literary Characterization of Mothers and Sexual Politics in the Hebrew Bible," Esther Fuchs shows brilliantly how the narratives about originally barren women and related texts reinforce the values of a patriarchal system. This essay is not an exercise in pointing out the blatant sexism of obviously misogynist texts. It is striking precisely because it shows how even texts that seem to present women as mature and independent agents are in fact elements in a network of social control.

In her other essay, "Who Is Hiding the Truth? Deceptive Women and Biblical Androcentrism," Ms. Fuchs shows that the majority of the female characters in the Hebrew Bible are presented as deceptive women. On a literary level, she argues that this portrayal is a patriarchal ideological tool which leads to the suspicion and distrust of women and which justifies their subordination. Insofar as female deception reflects historical reality, it results from the fact that in patriarchal systems, women are often barred from direct action. The real deception is committed by the androcentric text which ignores or suppresses the underlying motivations of powerless women.

The essays in this volume show clearly that historical-critical scholarship and feminism are not exclusive alternatives. Feminist biblical interpretation cannot do without historical-critical methods. In cases where feminist approaches bring other methods to bear, they are not unique in demonstrating the fruitfulness of complementary or even alternative methods. Historical-criticism has always claimed to be critical of the text and to approach it without bias or at least with self-consciousness about biases. Feminists are challenging historical critics to be faithful to that tradition, to become aware of and to correct androcentric bias both in themselves as interpreters and in the texts. It would seem then that the current tension between historical criticism and feminism is a creative one, a tension that leads us to be hopeful about the possibility of new insights into the texts as well as about the possibility of social transformation.

1

AMERICAN WOMEN AND THE BIBLE:
THE NATURE OF WOMAN AS A HERMENEUTICAL ISSUE

Carolyn De Swarte Gifford

For over three and one-half centuries the Christian faith and its sacred book, the Bible, have been a shaping influence in the lives of American women. Americans have turned to the scriptures for insight into the nature of womanhood, certain that they would find in biblical passages God's revelation concerning women, their duties, and their proper sphere. Countless sermons prescribing womanly behavior have been preached from biblical texts. Numerous books and articles of advice for young ladies employed biblical examples of the good woman and her evil opposite. Common speech borrowed biblical phrases to describe womanly attributes. It was both appropriate and inevitable for Americans, a Bible-reading people, to refer to the scriptures for definitions of female and male, ideals of woman- and manhood, and models of activity befitting Christian women and men.

By the late eighteenth and the early nineteenth century a small but growing number of women and men began to reflect on the biblical notion of womanhood, questioning whether traditional scriptural interpretations of the nature of woman did justice to God or to God's creation—woman. Throughout the nineteenth and twentieth centuries the debate over the biblical understanding of womanhood continued, affecting not only religion but all other institutions of American life. Wherever that debate has been carried on—whether politely through articles in denominational magazines on women's right to be delegates to church bodies or in the much more highly charged setting of women's suffrage conventions—the argument has been essentially over the same basic issue: hermeneutics. How shall the scriptures be interpreted and who shall interpret them? These same questions have been raised over and over again in relation to "the woman question," and they have been answered in different ways by various segments of American society. The issue remains unresolved to the present day, as conflicting notions of womanhood and woman's sphere prevail in different religious communities and are reflected in their members' attitudes toward legislative issues, court decisions, business practices, etc. which affect women.

At the close of the eighteenth century a Massachusetts woman, Judith Sargent Murray, wrote an essay entitled "On the Equality of the Sexes" (1790). In it she sought to build a case for opening up more educational opportunities to women since, in her opinion, they were endowed by their creator with minds as sharp as men's. She appended to the body of her essay a letter she had written a decade earlier to a male friend who had attacked her egalitarian stance. He claimed male superiority in intelligence, as in all things, basing his claim on scriptural evidence. Murray replied:

> Not long since, weak and presuming as I was, I amused myself with selecting some arguments from nature, reason and experience, against this so generally received idea [of male superiority]. I confess that to the sacred testimonies I had not recourse. I held them to be merely metaphorical, and thus regarding them, I could not persuade myself that there was any propriety in bringing them to decide in this *very important debate*. However, as you, sir, confine yourself entirely to the sacred oracles, I mean to bend the whole of my artillery against those supposed proofs, which you have thence provided, and from which you have formed an intrenchment *apparently* so invulnerable.[1]

Murray never actually developed an extended counterargument in her letter to meet her friend's scriptural proofs of male superiority. Yet their exchange anticipated issues that would become significant in the following two centuries of discussion on the rights of women.

Murray recognized that it would be necessary for supporters of women's equality to give scriptural justifications for their position since debates were likely to be couched in these terms. She had believed that "arguments from nature, reason and experience" were sufficient to make her point. Her friend's appeals to "sacred oracles," however, alerted her to the fact that biblical proofs were often adduced in debate. While arguments such as Murray's might lend additional strength to a particular position, proofs from scripture held an unassailable authority for many.

Her somewhat facetious remarks indicate that Murray failed to realize precisely how seriously "sacred testimonies" were taken by Americans. She treated them lightly, dismissing them as "merely metaphorical" and not really worthy of being marshaled in support of the weighty matter of equal education for women. When her opponent invoked a traditional argument claiming that Eve's disobedience in the Garden of

---

[1] Judith Sargent Murray, "On the Equality of the Sexes," as quoted in *The Feminist Papers* (ed. Alice S. Rossi; New York: Bantam, 1974) 22–23; emphasis in original.

Eden had caused the Fall and provoked God to decree women's subordination to man in punishment for her sin, Murray responded with her own interpretation of the Adam and Eve story. She suggested that Adam as well as Eve had defied God by eating the fruit from the tree of the knowledge of good and evil. But whereas Eve was motivated by a laudable desire to gain more knowledge, Adam, in accepting Eve's invitation to eat the apple, acted only out of "bare pusillanimous attachment to a woman!"[2] Murray regarded this motive as far less praiseworthy than Eve's hunger to know more.

Because Murray viewed the scriptural account as metaphorical and thus capable of conveying not only different levels of meaning but also of bearing more than one possibility of interpretation, she saw nothing questionable in using the Garden of Eden story as a vehicle for her own musings on the nature of women and men. In doing so she recognized what biblical scholars a century and a half later would understand as the mythopoeic quality of the book of Genesis. For her friend, however, as for a large portion of Americans from the eighteenth century to the present, scripture—particularly key passages such as Gen 3:16, a favorite proof text for the justification of woman's subordination to man—did not admit of more than one meaning.

Furthermore that meaning was to be assigned by male clergy and not by females, no matter how clever and witty they might think themselves. It was not appropriate for women to interpret the texts since that would disturb the traditional notion of male domination. Expounding the meaning of scripture was a solemn task, not to be undertaken with any hint of levity. Murray and others later on, such as Elizabeth Cady Stanton, who criticized traditional patriarchal understanding of the Bible, may have offended nearly as much by their apparently frivolous attitude as by their attacks on conventional scriptural interpretation. For most people the Bible was no laughing matter and to suggest that there might be a humorous aspect to hermeneutical issues was seen as disrespectful and, worse, irreverent.

As the nineteenth century began, women continued the demand for equal schooling for girls begun by Judith Sargent Murray as part of a broader push to educate all children of the young republic. Democratic ideals required that all citizens be intellectually equipped to participate in government. Women, no less than men, needed education in order to train their sons for responsible citizenship. Although it was understood that women would not themselves provide leadership in America's political and economic life—since they must, of course, remain subordinate to men in such matters—they could teach future leaders, not only as mothers but also as school mistresses, a profession opening up for women by the

[2] Ibid., 24.

early nineteenth century. While women could not govern, they could guide, and their guidance extended to the moral and religious realms. Women filled the ranks of teachers in the newly developing Sunday schools as well as public schools, exerting spiritual and moral influence over America's youth. Woman's role as moral arbiter became enshrined as a facet of what contemporary feminist historians refer to as the Cult of True Womanhood.[3] This cult hallowed woman in her proper sphere, centering on the private world of home and church (increasingly understood during the period as an extension of the private world). It was perfectly acceptable for women to take on the duty of children's moral education; in fact it was seen as necessary since men were busy in their proper sphere, the public world, increasingly concerned with political and economic duties. If women could impart ethical precepts while remaining suitably submissive, such activity would not threaten the orderly arrangement of male and female spheres which Americans had come to believe was God-ordained and revealed in the Bible.

With the wave of reform activity sweeping the country in the second quarter of the century a few brave women began to extend their role as moral arbiters beyond their prescribed sphere. In the 1830s female abolitionists like Angelina Grimké and Abby Kelley Foster began to speak before "promiscuous assemblies"—public gatherings of both males and females—pleading the cause of the slave. In 1840 Lucretia Mott and other women antislavery leaders expected to be seated with the American delegations at the World's Anti-Slavery Convention in London. By the 1850s reformers in favor of temperance, like Susan B. Anthony, rose to voice their opinions in rallies and conferences. Communities of reformers were forced to examine the notion of woman's proper sphere and the biblical undergirding for it.

An early example of the tension between the ideal of woman's domestic sphere and her role as moral arbiter can be seen in the clash between the Grimké sisters, Angelina and Sarah, and the Massachusetts clergy. These southern Quaker women had been speaking against slavery throughout the Northeast, sponsored by abolition societies. Their public role prompted a strongly worded "Pastoral Letter (from) the General Association of Massachusetts to the Churches Under Their Care" (1837), condemning such activities. It is worth quoting at length because it so clearly sets forth opinion current in New England "Orthodoxy" (Congregationalism) about woman's proper sphere and duties, an opinion grounded in a widely held interpretation of scripture, one still voiced today in some segments of American society:

[3] Barbara Welter, "The Cult of True Womanhood: 1800–1860," *Dimity Convictions: The American Woman in the Nineteenth Century* (Athens, OH: Ohio University Press, 1976).

The appropriate duties and influence of woman are clearly stated in the New Testament. Those duties and that influence are unobtrusive and private, but the source of mighty power. . . . The power of woman is her dependence, flowing from the consciousness of that weakness which God has given her for her protection, and which keeps her in those departments of life that form the character of individuals, and of the nation. There are social influences which females can use in promoting piety and the great objects of Christian benevolence which we can not too highly recommend.

We appreciate the unostentatious prayers and efforts of woman in advancing the cause of religion at home and abroad; in Sabbath Schools; in leading religious inquirers to the pastors for instruction; and in all such associated effort as becomes the modesty of her sex. . . . But when she assumes the place and tone of man as a public reformer, our care and protection of her seem unnecessary; we put ourselves in self-defence against her; she yields the power which God has given her for her protection, and her character becomes unnatural. . . . We can not, therefore, but regret the mistaken conduct of those who encourage females to bear an obtrusive and ostentatious part in measures of reform, and countenance any of that sex who so far forget themselves as to itinerate in the character of public lecturers and teachers.[4]

For the Massachusetts Orthodox (Congregational) clergy the crucial issue was the male/public realm versus the female/private realm. In their opinion female abolitionists (and, later, female temperance reformers and women's rights advocates) overstepped the boundary of the private realm to which God had confined woman. Thus the debate in this instance was not over abolitionism, since some of the Massachusetts clergy supported the antislavery cause. But the spectacle of women defying both God and Saint Paul by their public appearances on behalf of abolition was a horrible one for these clergymen to contemplate. Indeed such women were "unnatural," unwomanly, even monstrous. Throughout the nineteenth and twentieth centuries, those opposing a public role for women used the threat of unnaturalness to frighten women who dared to cross the border from private to public. Scripturally derived epithets such as "disobedient Eve" and "Jezebel woman" were hurled at women and often such name-calling was enough to discourage the more timid from venturing beyond the private realm. Biblical images carried within them enormous capacity to inhibit, as those who employed them knew well. Disobedient Eves challenged not only men but also God; they were not merely stubborn and headstrong but sinful as well. Women's rights reformers would have to develop alternative female biblical images that would empower women, rather than repress

---

[4] "Pastoral Letter (from) the General Association of Massachusetts to the Churches Under Their Care," quoted in *The Feminist Papers*, 305–6. See also Alice S. Rossi's introductory section on women and reform in the nineteenth century (pp. 241–81).

them.[5] The task of re-visioning images begun in the nineteenth century still continues today.

In the meantime each small step over the boundary, however hesitant, brought into question the whole concept of separate spheres.[6] Although Angelina Grimké and Abby Kelley Foster were often shouted down in antislavery meetings, many heard them and were persuaded to the cause of abolition. Although Lucretia Mott and other women delegates from the United States to the World's Anti-Slavery Convention were not allowed to sit with their delegations, the incident provoked a young recruit to the cause, Elizabeth Cady Stanton, to plan a women's rights convention with her new friend Mrs. Mott. They issued a call for the first such meeting eight years later at Seneca Falls, New York. And although Susan B. Anthony was refused permission to speak to rallies of temperance supporters, such a refusal merely served as what twentieth-century feminists would term consciousness-raising events, making them more firmly committed to the struggle for women's rights than they had been previously. The leadership of the nineteenth-century women's rights movement sharpened its reasoning and rhetorical skills through combatting traditional scriptural views of woman's place. In the process they began to formulate new interpretations of scripture.

The New Testament texts to which the Pastoral Letter referred included such passages as 1 Cor 11:3–12 and 14:34–35, Eph 5:22–24, 1 Tim 2:9–15, and 1 Pet 3:1–7, which were continually cited as proof texts for the subordination of women and the circumscribing of their proper sphere. The Grimkés countered with proof texts of their own, passages such as Gal 3:28, which they used to support their view of women as responsible moral beings created equal by God and endowed with consciences capable of being roused against injustice and oppression. When confronted with such clear examples of injustice as slavery in the South and racism in the North, women as well as men must use any means consonant with their consciences to fight these evils.[7]

The struggle over the position of women in the light of scripture often seems to have been carried on by combatants only by means of

---

[5] See Carolyn De Swarte Gifford ("Home Protection: The WCTU's Conversion to Woman Suffrage" [unpublished manuscript, 1980]) for a discussion of revisioning images and symbols and the power of symbols to repress.

[6] See Dorothy C. Bass, "'Their Prodigious Influence': Women, Religion and Reform in Ante-Bellum America," *Women of Spirit: Female Leadership in the Jewish and Christian Traditions* (ed. Rosemary Ruether and Eleanor McLaughlin; New York: Simon & Schuster, 1979); and Carolyn De Swarte Gifford, "Women and Social Reform," *Women and Religion in America: The Nineteenth Century* (ed. Rosemary Radford Ruether and Rosemary Skinner Keller; New York: Harper & Row, 1981).

[7] Angelina Emily Grimké, *Letters to Catharine Beecher* (Boston: Isaac Knapp, 1836) 118. See also Letter XI.

spouting opposing proof texts at each other. Yet many of the participants throughout the nineteenth and twentieth centuries were also suggesting, however obliquely, that there could be different criteria for interpreting scripture underlying the choice of opposing proof texts. The Pastoral Letter of the Massachusetts clergy is an example of an interpretation of scripture that took as a guiding principle or criterion the notion that God from creation intended that females be subordinate to males and that they inhabit different spheres. Developing a different criterion, the Grimkés, like many abolitionists, were convinced that the central scriptural message was one of liberation from oppression.

In Angelina Grimké's *Appeal to the Christian Women of the South* (1836), she suggested that southern women could do four things to overthrow slavery: read, pray, speak out, and act. Their reading material should be the scriptures, which they ought to approach "in the spirit of inquiry and the spirit of prayer. . . . Read the *Bible* then, it contains the words of Jesus, and they are spirit and life. Judge for yourselves whether *he sanctioned* such a system of oppression and crime."[8] The freeing message and acts of Jesus were, for Grimké and others, the criterion by which to interpret the rest of the Bible and to judge one's own ethical choices. The theme of freedom from oppression, which antislavery reformers believed so strongly dominated both the Old and the New Testament, was accompanied by an equally strong subtheme: speaking the truth in defiance of public opinion, the religious hierarchy, and the laws of one's country. Grimké saw the Bible from beginning to end peopled with prophets, apostles, and martyrs willing to suffer for the sake of truth. Abolitionists were the latest in a long line of such persons who could be traced from biblical times to the present, and among those courageous souls were women.

Grimké listed the valiant women of the Bible: Miriam, Deborah, Jael, Huldah, Esther, Elizabeth, Anna, the Samaritan woman, the company of women who followed Jesus to the Cross, Mary the Mother of Jesus, Mary Magdalene, the women on whom the Holy Spirit descended at Pentecost, and the women mentioned by Paul who taught and ministered to the earliest Christian communities. All sorts of women's rights reformers throughout the nineteenth and twentieth centuries— those who worked for equality for women in the churches as well as in the larger society—would lift up these biblical women as models for their own public activity and gain inspiration from their courageous example to persist with reform in the face of ridicule and persecution. For women reformers the Bible evidenced no such differentiated spheres and gender roles in the task of reforming the world as the Massachusetts

[8] Angelina Emily Grimké, *Appeal to the Christian Women of the South* (New York: Arno and New York Times, 1969; original 1836) 17; emphasis in original.

clergy defended in their Pastoral Letter.

As people chose opposing sides in the controversy over woman's proper sphere, they began to develop alternative interpretations of scripture stemming from different interpretive criteria and appealing to different sets of biblical passages. Those who believed in separate spheres and complementary but unequal roles for male and female articulated what has come to be known as a "subordinationist" or hierarchical interpretation of male–female relationships as found in scripture. They appealed to the second account of creation (Genesis 2 and 3, particularly 2:22); portraits in the Old Testament of good (obedient) wives and bad (disobedient) women; and to the passages in the New Testament epistles cited above, all of which seemed to them to teach the subordination of women. Those who found in the Bible the central theme of freedom from oppression and a more egalitarian view of male–female relationships cited the first account of creation (Genesis 1, particularly 1:26–27); tales of heroic women of scripture; passages indicating that the Holy Spirit empowered both women and men (especially Acts 2:17–18); and Gal 3:28, perhaps the most popular text of women's rights reformers.

The debate over women's proper activities in movements of reform led immediately to an examination of woman's subordinate status in American society generally. Angelina Grimké's sister Sarah replied directly to the Massachusetts clergy's Pastoral Letter in a series of letters of her own, printed together in a widely read collection, "Letters on the Equality of the Sexes and the Condition of Women" (1837). She insisted that Americans face the serious contradiction between the notion of female subordination and the biblical principles of freedom and equality. Like many Americans, Sarah Grimké believed that the nation had been founded on these principles. Struggles for abolition and other reform activities were carried out in order to enable America to embody its ideals. Slaves must be freed if her country was to live up to its high calling, she reasoned, and if slaves, so also women must be freed.

Grimké began her discourse on woman's equality by announcing that she would base her arguments on scripture. In doing so she would be countering a false interpretation of biblical truths:

> My dear friend,—in attempting to comply with thy request to give my views on the Province of Woman, I feel that I am venturing on nearly untrodden ground, and that I shall advance arguments in opposition to a corrupt public opinion, and to the perverted interpretation of Holy Writ, which has so universally obtained. . . . In examining this important subject I shall depend solely on the Bible to designate the sphere of woman, because I believe that almost every thing that has been written on this subject, has been the result of a misconception of the simple

> truths revealed in the Scriptures, in consequence of the false
> translation of many passages of Holy Writ.[9]

According to Grimké, the whole concept of the subordination of women
was based on a fundamental and willful misunderstanding of the original, inspired biblical texts. God did not intend to make women subordinate to men. Male translators and interpreters of the Bible introduced
the mistaken notion because it reflected the cultures in which they lived
and undergirded their own opinions on what normative relationships
between males and females should be. Unfortunately for women, it became the basis for the definition of womanhood and woman's sphere
that prevailed.

This false interpretation was not only enshrined in the teaching of
the churches but also embedded in the mores of so-called Christian societies such as the United States, making it necessary to mount a full-scale
onslaught against the unjust subjugation of women like the one that abolitionists had already launched against slavery. Grimké called for nothing
less than the overturning of centuries of oppression against women by a
return to the true teaching about womanhood to be found in what she
held to be the original biblical message of freedom and equality.

Like her sister Angelina and many other Quakers, Sarah Grimké
believed that in Jesus' teachings one could best grasp the egalitarian,
liberating theme of the Bible. But whereas Angelina Grimké had, at first,
judged only the institution of slavery by the criterion of Jesus' teachings,
Sarah Grimké extended that judgment to the institutionalized relationships between men and women. She wrote:

> The Lord Jesus defines the duties of his followers in his Sermon
> on the Mount. He lays down grand principles by which they
> should be governed, without any reference to sex or condi-
> tion. . . . I follow him through all his precepts, and find him
> giving the same directions to women as to men, never even refer-
> ring to the distinction now so strenuously insisted upon between
> masculine and feminine virtues: this is one of the anti-christian
> "traditions of men" which are taught instead of the "command-
> ments of God." Men and women were CREATED EQUAL: they
> are both moral and accountable beings, and whatever is *right* for
> man to do, is *right* for woman.[10]

Thus, for Grimké, the Pastoral Letter of the Massachusetts clergy in its
insistence on different spheres and duties for men and women supported
"anti-Christian 'traditions of men'" and not the "commandments of God."

If false teachings about women had been disseminated through incor-
rect translations and biased interpretations of scripture, then different

---

[9] Sarah M. Grimké, *Letters on the Equality of the Sexes and the Condition of Woman*
(New York: Burt Franklin, 1970; original 1838) 3–4.
[10] Ibid., 16; emphasis in original.

translations and interpretations must be produced which would remain true to the original inspiration of the Bible. Since Grimké had serious doubts about men's ability to carry on such activity without bias, she called for women to do the work. However, she recognized that in order to prepare themselves they must learn Hebrew and Greek, and she did not imagine that women would be admitted either quickly or easily to the study of biblical languages.

Yet a few women were already planning such study, among them Lucy Stone, who was a nineteen-year-old Massachusetts school teacher in 1837 when Grimké wrote her *Letters on the Equality of the Sexes.* As a child, Stone had been horrified by biblical injunctions against women and decided to discover for herself what the Bible really taught in regard to women. She found particularly troubling the segment of Gen 3:16—"Thy desire shall be to thy husband, and he shall rule over thee" (KJV)—popularly known as "the curse of Eve." Stone's mother had explained to her daughter that it was woman's duty to submit to this curse since all women shared in Eve's disobedience and her consequent fallenness. Women's subordinate status was not only part of the order of creation but was also deserved punishment for original sin. Like Lucy Stone's mother, most women humbly accepted what they believed to be God's commandment of submissiveness, but Stone would not do so. She determined to read the Bible in the original languages and entered Oberlin College in 1843 to study Hebrew and Greek. Although Stone did not continue her language work beyond college, she did become a leading women's rights reformer in the nineteenth century, being convinced that there was absolutely no biblical basis for women's subordination.

The traditional translation and interpretation of Gen 3:16 had already been disputed before Stone began her language studies. Sarah Grimké and others even earlier had pointed out that with an alternative translation of verb forms—from "shall" to "will"—the passage could be read as God's prediction of women's lot in a fallen creation rather than God's timeless commandment for women. If the meaning of a text so crucial to a subordinationist view of women could be radically altered by changing one word, it might be possible to reinterpret other passages used to restrict women, thus bringing the whole scriptural underpinning for the position into question. Grimké proceeded to do this: she cited further alternative translations and interpretations of other favorite proof texts for women's subordination, drawing upon the work of earlier Quaker scholars who had provided the biblical foundation for their denomination's unprecedented egalitarian treatment of women.[11]

Throughout the next several decades, women continued to call for what might now be termed a feminist exegesis of the Bible. Beginning with

[11] Ibid., Letters I–IV, XI, XIV.

the Seneca Falls Convention of 1848, a series of women's rights meetings provided a dramatic and well-publicized forum for discussion of the role that the Bible and religious institutions played in the oppression of women. The call to the first convention clearly stated that inquiry into "the religious condition and rights of woman" as well as their social and civil status would be central on the agenda. A "Declaration of Sentiments," produced by the convention organizers and enthusiastically adopted by those attending, listed among the wrongs committed against women their exclusion from the ministry, from the teaching of theology, and from virtually all public participation in church governance. A resolution unanimously passed by the body succinctly captured the stance toward the Bible and its relation to women taken by the leadership of the women's rights movement almost to the end of the century: "*Resolved*, That woman has too long rested satisfied in the circumscribed limits which corrupt customs and a perverted application of the Scriptures have marked out for her, and that it is time she should move in the enlarged sphere which her great Creator has assigned her."[12] Almost without exception women's rights leaders in the nineteenth century firmly believed that the Bible, correctly interpreted, would disclose God's intention that women be equal to men. Although generations of men might be sexist, God was not. They rather naively assumed that it was simply a matter of encouraging unbiased investigation of the Bible by scholars and nonscholars alike, in order to change American society's definition of womanhood and woman's sphere.

The growth of the scholarly discipline of biblical criticism during the nineteenth century gave promise of developing presuppositions and interpretive tools that might allow a feminist exegesis. Those women's rights supporters who called for new translations and interpretations of the Bible did so implicitly in opposition to the notion of the plenary inspiration of scripture, in which the majority of the American public as well as ministers and theological professors believed. Charles Hodge, professor at Princeton Seminary and champion of Protestant orthodoxy, clearly stated the meaning of the phrase "plenary inspiration" in his work *Systematic Theology* published in 1873: "The Scriptures of the Old and New Testaments are the Word of God, written under the inspiration of the Holy Spirit, and therefore infallible and of divine authority in all things pertaining to faith and practice, and consequently free from all error, whether of doctrines, fact, or precept."[13] However staunchly the

---

[12] Mari Jo and Paul Buhle, *The Concise History of Woman Suffrage: Selections from the Classic Work of Stanton, Anthony, Gage and Harper* (Urbana, IL: University of Illinois Press, 1978) 91.

[13] Charles Hodge, *Systematic Theology*, 1. 152, quoted in Ira V. Brown "Higher Criticism Comes to America, 1880–1900," *Journal of Presbyterian History* 38 (1960) 194. See also Aileen S. Kraditor, *The Ideas of the Woman Suffrage Movement, 1890–1920* (Garden City, NY: Doubleday, 1971) chap. 4.

majority held to the notion of the inerrancy of the Bible, such belief was being shaken for many as the century progressed by several trends in Western intellectual thought, including biblical criticism.

So-called lower criticism—textual criticism that aimed at establishing the original text of scripture free from mistranslations—and higher criticism which sought to discover the historical background of the biblical texts, their authors, sources, and literary characteristics, had been rigorously pursued in Europe, particularly in Germany, since the late eighteenth century. By the 1870s German scholarship had convincingly demonstrated that the earlier books of the Old Testament were not authored by Moses, as orthodoxy had believed, but were, rather, a composite product of at least four different groups of authors (J, E, P, D) over a period of approximately five hundred years. Nineteenth-century work on the New Testament was attempting to establish the times in which the various books had been written, the authorship of the Gospel of John, and the relationships between the synoptic gospels.

American scholars were aware of the findings of biblical criticism as early as the second decade of the century, when liberal Unitarian professors at Harvard and more conservative colleagues at Andover Seminary discussed, debated, and taught biblical criticism and founded journals devoted to disseminating the results of the latest biblical scholarship. Americans traveled to Germany to study higher criticism at centers of biblical research such as Göttingen, Tübingen, Leipzig, Heidelberg, and Berlin. They returned home to teach what they had learned to successive generations of university and seminary students and to set up departments within American academic institutions to perpetuate the scientific study of scripture. By the 1880s and 1890s there were several such departments in the United States. The Society of Biblical Literature and Exegesis, the professional society for biblical scholars, was founded in 1880.[14] By the 1880s, also, a Revised Version of the Bible, drawing on the work of textual critics, was published in the United States, the New Testament in 1881 and the Old Testament in 1885. The mere event of its publication made the general public aware that there were different versions of the Bible, some claiming to be more accurate than others, thus subtly undermining the notion of inerrancy.

More important for nineteenth-century feminists than the specific details of biblical scholarship were the presuppositions on which the discipline was based. The notion that the Bible was not supernaturally inspired but had evolved naturally over the course of centuries, that it was the historical record of peoples and not the "voice of God," that it could be studied

---

[14] See Ernest W. Saunders (*Searching the Scriptures: A History of the Society of Biblical Literature, 1880–1980* [Chico, CA: Scholars Press, 1982]) for a centennial history of the SBL.

like any other literary work in terms of various genres and its contents located in various historical contexts—all of these presuppositions brought into question the plenary inspiration of scripture. The view of many women's rights leaders was echoed by Heber Newton, Episcopalian popularizer of higher criticism, when he contended that the Bible, while it surely contained God's word, was not, in its entirety, God's word.[15] If these presuppositions were indeed so, there were ramifications extending far beyond the discipline of biblical criticism. Not only could biblical scholars freely pursue their task, but feminists working from those same presuppositions could seriously question biblical authority in the matter of woman's nature and sphere. Although nineteenth-century feminists were not professional biblical scholars, some of them were well aware of the presuppositions, methods, and findings of critical biblical research and on occasion referred to them to support and undergird their attack on traditional views of the authority of scripture and the subordinate position of women.

There was almost certainly no conscious alliance of feminists and biblical scholars during the period. Yet the very existence of a group of serious researchers at work on higher biblical criticism, a growing collection of popular works on the subject, and an increasing number of clergy preaching who were trained in higher critical methods and findings served to provide an intellectual climate somewhat more receptive to a view of the Bible which was at first profoundly disturbing to Americans. That it was disturbing is evidenced by several sensational heresy trials in the 1890s involving biblical scholars. Yet even the trials provided a forum for new views on the Bible. As Henry Preserved Smith of Lane Seminary, one of those tried, observed: "I can truly say that litigation was not to my taste, but I thought it was my duty to carry the case through for its educational value. The wide attention given to my case . . . would help some minds to a better, that is, a more historical, view of the Bible."[16] In much the same way, people who might be "helped to a better view" of the Bible might also be prompted to reexamine some of the traditional attitudes toward women grounded in a correspondingly traditional attitude toward the authority of scripture. Like others before them, women's rights leaders called for such a reexamination in the closing decades of the nineteenth century. But unlike the earlier generation, feminists at the end of the century could point to a growing body of biblical criticism which made possible new approaches to the Bible.

One of those calling for reinterpretation of the scriptural teaching on women in light of the new scholarship was Frances Willard (1839–1898), longtime president of the Women's Christian Temperance Union

---

[15] Brown, "Higher Criticism Comes to America," 206.
[16] Henry P(reserved) Smith, *The Heretic's Defense: A Footnote to History*, p. 48 (as quoted in Brown, "Higher Criticism Comes to America," 205).

(WCTU), who sought biblical sanction for an enlarged sphere for women, including equal rights for women within the church. Willard came out of an evangelical Protestant background as did the majority of the powerful organization she led. Many of these temperance women had participated in the mass revival meetings led by Dwight L. Moody during the 1870s, and earlier in the prayer groups and camp meetings of the Holiness movement. Willard herself had been converted at a Holiness revival by Phoebe Palmer (1807–1874), a leader of the movement. In a remarkable book, *The Promise of the Father* (1859), Palmer defended women's call to preach.[17] Although Palmer subscribed to a thoroughly traditional and conservative view of woman's nature and sphere, she cited three biblical passages—Joel 2:28, John 1:4, and Acts 2:17–18—which promised that in "the latter days" God's Holy Spirit would be poured out on women as well as men, enabling those extraordinary persons inspired by the Spirit to preach and prophesy. Unlike the Grimkés and others, she did not claim women's right to preach based on the idea that women were equal to men in the sight of God and should not inhabit a separate sphere from men. She insisted, rather, that under inspiration of the Holy Spirit some women might be called to step beyond their proper sphere temporarily and witness to God, returning to that sphere when the moment of inspiration passed.

Grounding the possibility of women's preaching on scriptural texts predicting and describing the inspiration of the Holy Spirit might not seem a particularly fruitful avenue of approach for those defending women's equal rights within the church. Angelina Grimké had pointed this out over two decades earlier in 1837, as she criticized her own sect, the Quakers, for using an argument similar to Phoebe Palmer's in their justification of women's preaching: "Women are regarded [among the Quakers] as equal to men on the ground of *spiritual gifts, not* on the broad ground of *humanity.* Woman may *preach*; this is a *gift*; but woman must *not* make the discipline by which *she herself* is governed."[18] And Phoebe Palmer did not seek for women's rights within the church, asking instead only that women who were truly inspired by the Spirit be allowed to preach and prophesy as did inspired men. Yet during the second half of the nineteenth century, offshoots of the Holiness movement sought to enlarge woman's sphere and provide for women's rights within the church and often called for them within the larger society as well.[19] In the same manner, many

---

[17] Phoebe Palmer, *The Promise of the Father, or A Neglected Speciality of the Last Days* (Boston: Henry V. Degen, 1859).

[18] Letter from Angelina Grimké to Theodore Weld and John Greenleaf Whittier, 30 March 1837, *Letters of Theodore Dwight Weld, Angelina Grimké Weld and Sarah Grimké* (ed. Edith H. Barnes and Dwight L. Dumond; Gloucester, MA: Peter Smith, 1965) 431; emphasis in original.

[19] For discussions of the biblical bases of evangelical feminism, see Donald W. Dayton,

WCTU orators and other women involved in the newly created women's missionary societies justified their moves beyond prescribed roles and activities by understanding themselves as participating in a "second Pentecost" in which God demanded new things from women. They saw the end of the nineteenth century as a time of a fresh outpouring of the power of the Holy Spirit—the "latter days" in which women would be empowered by God, in fulfillment of Joel's prophecy, as Palmer had suggested in her book.

Although Palmer and other conservative evangelical women did not believe that women should seek ordination and full lay rights within the church and certainly should not step beyond their proper sphere by demanding suffrage and other rights in the larger society, only one generation later Frances Willard did. She insisted that in "this new day for woman" she should seek a larger sphere, including suffrage and other political and civil rights, full laity rights within the churches, and the right to preach and be fully ordained.[20] Willard had personal experience of the limited sphere which the churches assigned to women. In 1880 the General Conference of the Methodist Episcopal Church (North) refused to allow her to speak, although she attended as a "fraternal delegate" from the rapidly growing and powerful WCTU. In 1888 the General Conference voted not to allow the seating of Willard and four other duly elected women delegates. In the midst of Willard's struggles for women's rights within the churches, she wrote *Woman in the Pulpit*, which called once again for women's exegesis:

> We need women commentators to bring out the women's side of the book; we need the stereoscopic view of truth in general, which can only be had when woman's eye and man's together shall discern the perspective of the Bible's full-orbed revelation. I do not at all impugn the good intention of the good men who have been our exegetes, and I bow humbly in presence of their scholarship; but, while they turn their linguistic telescopes on truth, I may be allowed to make a correction for the "personal equation" in the results which they espy.[21]

Discovering an Evangelical Heritage (New York: Harper & Row, 1976) chap. 8, "The Evangelical Roots of Feminism," and Nancy Hardesty, Lucille Sider Dayton, and Donald W. Dayton, "Women in the Holiness Movement: Feminism in the Evangelical Tradition," in *Women of Spirit*, ed. R. Ruether and E. McLaughlin.

[20] For discussions of biblical arguments for and against women's rights within the church, see Barbara Brown Zikmund, "The Feminist Thrust of Sectarian Christianity," in *Women of Spirit*, ed. R. Ruether and E. McLaughlin; idem, "The Struggle for the Right to Preach," in *Women and Religion in America*, ed. R. Ruether and R. S. Keller; and idem, "Biblical Arguments and Women's Place in the Church," in *The Bible and Social Reform* (ed. Ernest R. Sandeen; Chico, CA: Scholars Press, 1982).

[21] Frances E. Willard, *Woman in the Pulpit* (Chicago: Woman's Temperance Publication Association, 1889) 21.

Willard meant that male interpreters of scripture held a traditional view of woman's nature and sphere which did not allow them to take a fresh, unbiased look at the material in the texts, although they might sincerely believe that they were doing so. On the other hand, women exegetes, presumably those in particular who were interested in a less restricted position for women, could provide such an unbiased look. For example, Willard found in 1 Corinthians evidence that women did speak and prophesy in the early church, but she warned that such evidence will "hardly be emphasized as we could wish until women share equally in translating the sacred text." Echoing Sarah Grimké nearly a half century earlier, she urged "young women of linguistic talent . . . to make a specialty of Hebrew and New Testament Greek in the interest of their sex."[22]

She further accused men of exegeting scripture in such a way that Christianity "today imposes the heaviest yoke now worn by women upon that most faithful follower of Him who is her emancipator no less than humanity's Saviour."[23] In other words, Christianity had become the instrument of women's subordination contrary to the message and work of the savior it proclaimed. Willard stated explicitly what others before her had only implied, that "universal liberty of person and opinion are now conceded to be Bible-precept principles," and that if one came to the text with those principles in mind one would find instead of a restrictive view of woman's sphere, a liberating word for women which could help to bring them into full equality with men. Willard located this "Bible-precept of universal liberty of person and opinion" in the person of Jesus—his teaching and his action—as indicated in the above quotation which describes Jesus as "woman's emancipator."

Writing as she did in 1888, Willard nonetheless came close to what contemporary feminists suggest as the locus of a theology of liberation for women. For example, if one substitutes Rosemary Radford Ruether's phrase "central and critical norms which biblical religion applies to itself within its own context" for Willard's phrase "Bible-precept principles" one would approximate what Willard was trying to say.[24] For Willard, Jesus the Emancipator is that central, critical norm by which scripture is to be judged. She believed that "as the world becomes more deeply permeated by the principles of Christ's Gospel, methods of exegesis are revised. The old texts stand there just as before, but we interpret them less narrowly."[25] That is, one critiques biblical passages that present women as subordinate in the light of the freeing activity of Jesus Christ.

When Willard called for young women to learn biblical languages

---

[22] Ibid., 31.
[23] Ibid., 23.
[24] Rosemary Radford Ruether, "Feminism and Patriarchal Religion: Principles of Ideological Critique of the Bible," *Journal for the Study of the Old Testament* 22 (1982) 55.
[25] Willard, *Woman in the Pulpit*, 23.

and to acquire theological educations to apply the critical norm she saw in Jesus, she was demanding what some have termed "interested scholarship," research with a reformist purpose and point of view shaping it—in this instance a feminist stance which would seek through scholarship to make a contribution to the women's rights movement. In this she would be unlike higher biblical critics of her day who typically saw themselves doing "pure research," using scientific principles and methodologies, with no interest in the outcome of the research other than that of "serving the truth." Willard pointed out in a quotation cited above that men did indeed come to the texts with biases, and, thus, she implicitly questioned one of the presuppositions of higher biblical criticism—scientific objectivity—although she did not elaborate on this in her writings. In raising the issue of the unacknowledged patriarchal stance of male translators and interpreters, Willard, in a far less theologically sophisticated way, anticipated the challenge made by contemporary feminist biblical scholars such as Elisabeth Schüssler Fiorenza against the claim made by many of their colleagues in the field that their work is value-neutral and objective.[26]

Willard was similar to many other women's rights reformers in the nineteenth century who also longed to see educated women apply themselves to learning the tools of higher criticism in order to critique the patriarchal religion found in the biblical texts by way of a non-patriarchal faith, which they believed could also be found in the texts. These women were convinced that the Bible did indeed contain expressions of a nonpatriarchal faith and that through applying textual, historical, and literary criticism to the textual material, such a faith would emerge as normative for biblical religion. This would mean that women could continue to be both Christians and feminists. Some version of this stance was espoused by the majority of feminists in the late nineteenth century.

A few women's rights leaders, among them Elizabeth Cady Stanton, editor of *The Woman's Bible*, and Matilda Joslyn Gage, author of *Woman, Church and State*, were definitely not sanguine about the possibility that the biblical record contained any such nonpatriarchal faith. In the appendix to Part II of *The Woman's Bible*, Stanton wrote:

> In plain English the Bible evidences a degrading teaching in regard to woman. Women try to shelter themselves under false translations, interpretations and symbolic meanings. It does not occur to them that men learned in the languages have revised the book many times, but make no changes in woman's position. . . . Though familiar with "the designs of God," trained in Biblical research and

---

[26] Elisabeth Schüssler Fiorenza, "Feminist Theology and New Testament Interpretation," *Journal for the Study of the Old Testament* 22 (1982) 33–35.

> higher criticism . . . yet they cannot twist out of the Old Testament
> or the New Testament a message of justice, liberty, or equality
> from God to the women of the nineteenth century.[27]

Agreeing with Stanton, Gage pointed to research by nineteenth-century archaeologists and explorers who brought to light traces of matriarchal civilizations ruthlessly supplanted by later patriarchal societies. Gage called for a rebellion by women against their repression under both church and state.[28]

In compiling *The Woman's Bible*, the method followed by Stanton and her Revising Committee, composed of women who were authors, editors, and ordained ministers, was to comment on all passages in both Testaments dealing with women. As this work progressed during the 1890s, Stanton came to the conclusion that patriarchy was the very foundation of the Judeo-Christian religion as it had evolved over time. Men in control of institutional religion, be they biblical scholars or ministers, would not make any changes in woman's position because if they should do so, "the bottom falls out of the whole Christian theology." They would not dare to apply the presuppositions, methodology, and findings of over a century of biblical criticism to the position of women as presented in the Bible because this would shake the theological bases of what Stanton might more accurately have termed orthodox or Calvinist theology. Although biblical scholars were beginning to identify and separate out different literary genres in the Bible, identifying some parts as mythological in character, Stanton felt that ordinary worshippers in the pews would never be introduced to the conclusions of such scholarship (although in fact they were in some more liberal congregations). Thus *The Woman's Bible*, which took many of the conclusions of biblical criticism and applied them to the biblical position on women,

> comes to the ordinary reader like a real benediction. It tells her
> that the good Lord did not write the Book; that the garden scene
> is a fable: that she is in no way responsible for the laws of the
> universe. The Christian scholars and scientists will not tell her
> this, for they see that she is the key to the situation. Take the
> snake, the fruit tree and the woman from the tableau, and we
> have no fall, no frowning Judge, no Inferno, no everlasting pun-
> ishment,—hence no need of a Savior. Thus the bottom falls out of
> the whole Christian theology. Here is the reason why in all the
> Biblical researches and higher criticisms, the scholars never touch
> the position of woman.[29]

[27] Elizabeth Cady Stanton et al., The Revising Committee, *The Woman's Bible*, Part II (New York: European, 1898) 214.

[28] Matilda Joslyn Gage, *Woman, Church and State: The Original Expose of Male Collaboration Against the Female Sex* (Watertown, MA: Persephone Press, 1980; original 1893) 7–23, 246.

[29] Elizabeth Cady Stanton, letter to *The Critic*, 3 March 1896. See Barbara Welter's

Stanton was clearly, by this time in her life and career (she was in her eighties), quite willing to let the bottom fall out of the traditional theology which had dominated American religion in one form or another from the seventeenth until the nineteenth century. She found her own religious faith in an eclectic and unsystematic combination of a number of trends of thought developing over the eighteenth and nineteenth centuries in reaction to traditional Calvinism, including Unitarian-Universalist beliefs, transcendentalism, free thought, and a benign form of social Darwinism.

Stanton was a thoroughgoing daughter of Enlightenment liberalism, who tended to judge the Bible not through its own critical norms as Willard would have women do but by the external norm of nineteenth-century liberal thought. At the close of the nineteenth century, she believed, Western civilization had progressed far beyond those earlier civilizations which produced the biblical record in terms of the understanding of the ideals of liberty, justice, and equality. Thus biblical notions should be measured against nineteenth-century liberalism, and when so measured, she implied over and over again in her own commentaries in *The Woman's Bible*, scripture would be found wanting in its teachings. Although it might contain ideas that represented a clear advancement over much of the conventional wisdom of the times in which it was written, it might itself be supplanted by ideals of later centuries.[30] Stanton's thinking here probably represented one of the most radical results of treating the Bible like any other book, one of the presuppositions of many proponents of higher biblical criticism. If the Judeo-Christian belief system was based fundamentally on the oppression of women, as Stanton insisted it was, then in the late nineteenth century it was an inadequate expression of the ideals of liberty, justice, and equality developed by that time. What women needed, she implied, was a different belief system, "a new 'rational religion' deliberately designed 'in harmony with science, common sense and the experience of mankind in natural laws,'" one which would embody the highest ideals of nineteenth-century culture, including as a principal tenet the equality of women in all areas of life.[31] In advocating such a system, Stanton differed fundamentally from

introduction to the Arno Press reprint of *The Woman's Bible*, "Something Remains to Dare" *(The Original Feminist Attack on the Bible* [New York: Arno Press, 1974]) for a presentation of *The Woman's Bible* as a product of changes in American religion during the nineteenth century and for a discussion of Stanton's own religious background.

[30] For examples of Stanton's contention that the ideals expressed in the Bible did not measure up to those of the nineteenth century, see *The Woman's Bible*, Part I, Stanton's commentary on Genesis, pp. 46, 60, 67; on Exodus, pp. 72–73; Part II, Preface, p. 8; Gospel of Mark, p. 131; 1 Corinthians, p. 158. Also see Elizabeth Cady Stanton, letter to the editor in *The Index*, 9 September 1876.

[31] Elizabeth Cady Stanton as quoted in Ellen Carol DuBois's critical commentary on excerpts from *The Woman's Bible* in *Elizabeth Cady Stanton and Susan B. Anthony: Correspondence, Writings, Speeches* (New York: Schocken Books, 1981) 228–29.

Frances Willard, who was still confident that the Bible—and thus Christianity—correctly understood by using the tools of higher criticism for the purpose might be shown to reveal the highest norms of liberty and equality.

If one were to have asked Elizabeth Cady Stanton if it was possible to be both a traditional Christian and a feminist, the answer would probably have been No. As she insisted, "[one] cannot twist out of the Old Testament or the New Testament [in plain English] a message of justice, liberty, or equality from God to the women of the nineteenth century." Apparently she had little hope that the biblical scholars and theologians of her time would undertake the revolutionary hermeneutical task involved in a thorough critique of theological concepts such as creation, sinfulness, and salvation as they had been interpreted for almost two millennia by male theologians.[32] The women's movement as well as professional biblical scholars and theologians failed to grapple with the implications of Stanton's claim that the Judeo-Christian tradition was sexist at its very core. Many women's rights leaders publicly repudiated *The Woman's Bible* and increasingly stepped back from a radical feminist critique of the interlocking institutional structures of religion, economics, and government which restricted women, to concentrate on more narrowly specific goals such as suffrage.

If Stanton was disappointed by the women's movement in her hope for a thorough examination of religion's role in institutionalized sexism, how much more disillusioned might Sarah Grimké and Frances Willard have been had they realized that the entry of trained women into the field of biblical scholarship would not result for nearly a century in the feminist hermeneutics they had demanded. Women began to join the ranks of professional biblical scholars shortly after the organization of the Society of Biblical Literature (SBL), the first woman's name appearing on the membership lists in 1894. However, their numbers were always small, never rising above 10 percent of the total membership and in most years considerably lower than that, and the results of their scholarship published in the journal of their professional association does not indicate that they were concerned with a feminist interpretation of scripture.[33] They do not seem

---

[32] See Beverly Wildung Harrison ("The Early Feminists and the Clergy: A Case Study in the Dynamics of Secularization," *The Review and Expositor* 73 [1975] 41–52) for a discussion of the tensions between evangelical clergy and women's rights leaders, among them Elizabeth Cady Stanton, which resulted in early feminists' disenchantment with their evangelical faith.

[33] For discussions of women's participation in the SBL and for a review of women's struggles during the nineteenth and twentieth centuries to obtain a theological education both outside of and within the seminaries, see Dorothy C. Bass, "Women's Studies and Biblical Studies: An Historical Perspective," *Journal for the Study of the Old Testament* 22 (1982) 6–12; and idem, "Women with a Past: A New Look at the History of Theologi-

to have made a "specialty of Hebrew and Greek in the interest of their sex," as Frances Willard would have wished.

Such activity continued to come from outside the profession in the work of such isolated scholars as the Reverend Lee Anna Starr, Methodist Protestant minister in Adrian, Michigan, in the early twentieth century, and Dr. Katherine Bushnell, former medical missionary to China and Women's Christian Temperance Union leader during the late nineteenth century. In the 1920s both women produced extended analyses of the treatment of women as recorded in the Bible and interpretations of the theological bases for woman's nature and sphere in the biblical texts, using their knowledge of biblical languages and scholarship.[34] Both concluded that the Bible correctly translated and interpreted presented a vision of the equality of women and men.

It was not until 1964 that a female professional biblical scholar raised the issue of male domination in the shaping of the Judeo-Christian tradition and urged women to assume an active role in the reshaping of the faith. In that year Margaret Brackenbury Crook, Professor of Religion and Biblical Literature at Smith College and thirty-nine-year member of the SBL, published *Women and Religion*. She proposed to carry out what she termed a "reconnaissance," a survey of women's position in Judaism and Christianity as reflected primarily in the biblical account, drawing on the results of the latest scholarship in her field as well as the disciplines of church history, theology, worship studies, and comparative religion. In her introduction, Crook made clear what she believed such a survey would reveal:

> A masculine monopoly in religion begins when Miriam raises her indignant question: "Does the Lord speak only through Moses?" Since then, in all three of the great religious groups stemming from the land and books of Israel—Judaism, Christianity, and Islam—men have formulated doctrine and established systems of worship offering only meager opportunity for expression of the religious genius of womankind. . . . If a woman born and bred in any of these faiths takes a comprehensive look at the form of theology best known to her, she discovers that it is masculine in

[34] Lee Anna Starr, *The Bible Status of Women* (New York: Fleming Revell, 1926); and Katherine C. Bushnell, *God's Word to Women* (no publishing information, but probably published privately by the author in Oakland, CA, 1923; reissued by Ray B. Munson, Box 52, North Collins, NY 14111); and idem, *The Reverend Doctor and his Doctor Daughter* (Oakland, CA: Katherine C. Bushnell, 1927). This last is a little known and often hilarious account of a dialogue between a rather stuffy clergyman and his physician daughter on the daughter's intention to follow in her father's footsteps by becoming ordained. His "conversion" to the daughter's point of view on the propriety of women being ordained follows rather swiftly after his daughter, using her medical skills, saves her father's life as he chokes on his false tooth which he has swallowed at the height of one of his impassioned arguments against women ministers.

administration, in the phrasing of its doctrines, liturgies, and
hymns. It is man-formulated, man-argued, man-directed.[35]

Crook repeatedly claimed that her intent was not "feminist" and she
meant to display no animosity toward men. She was simply stating the
facts of the case on the basis of overwhelming evidence, and those facts
clearly showed that women living within the influence of the three religious groups she named were still caught in a man's world. She felt that
although women in the United States had made rapid advances in many
fields during the twentieth century they had not made an impact on
religion. They must now move to the forefront in all areas of religious
life, particularly as theologians developing an adequate expression of the
"balanced partnership" of women and men which she envisioned for the
near future. She boldly asserted that the revolutionary scientific discover-
ies of the space age ought to stimulate equally new insights about the
nature of God and God's relationship to humankind, retaining fidelity to
the profound imagery within the biblical texts, yet phrased in a fresh
language produced through a dialogue of women and men. Crook imag-
ined new movements springing up within the Christian traditions in
response to challenges arising in the world, a time of turmoil, perhaps
even of crisis, yet offering opportunities for constructive change. And
women, she insisted, must participate in defining a changing Christian
tradition: "The time has come for women to share fully in creating the
basic structure of the thought that is to animate these movements, in the
forms of devotion, the art and symbolism that must be created to give
the new inspiration durability."[36] Crook understood well the necessity
that fundamental changes in a religious tradition must be reflected
through all aspects of that tradition, so she called for more than just a
new translation and interpretation of scripture.

The decade of the sixties saw other women questioning the adequacy
of "man-formulated" theology. Even earlier than Crook, theologian and
philosopher Valerie Saiving suggested in "The Human Situation: A Feminine View" (1960) that male theologians' definitions of key Judeo-Christian
concepts such as sin did not reflect or interpret women's experience and
thus needed to be rethought and reformulated in order to get at the depths
of meaning behind such concepts.[37] From outside the ranks of academia,
Elsie Culver, a professional lay church worker, pointed to the absence of a
significant body of research by modern biblical scholars on woman's status
and role in the cultures that produced the biblical texts and a discussion of

[35] Margaret Brackenbury Crook, *Women and Religion* (Boston: Beacon, 1964) 1, 5.
[36] Ibid., 247–48.
[37] Valerie Saiving (Goldstein), "The Human Situation: A Feminine View," in *Woman-spirit Rising: A Feminist Reader in Religion* (ed. Carol P. Christ and Judith Plaskow;
New York: Harper & Row, 1979) 27, 36–41.

what relevance findings from such research would have for contemporary women. She, like Crook and Saiving, felt that women had been excluded from the realm of theological discourse where the definition and interpretation of reality takes place.[38] If women did not share fully in such definition and interpretation they were relegated to second-class status. All three women were saying in the sixties what Mary Daly would articulate with such powerful imagery and sense of urgency in *Beyond God the Father* (1973): "We have not been free to use our own power to name ourselves, the world, or God. The old naming was not the product of dialogue. . . . Women are now realizing that the universal imposing of names by men has been false because partial."[39]

It was this power of naming, of sharing in the definition and interpretation of reality, for which Sarah and Angelina Grimké, Frances Willard, Elizabeth Cady Stanton, Matilda Joslyn Gage, and other nineteenth-century women longed. Although perhaps only Stanton and Gage would have been prepared to step with Daly beyond Christianity in search of self-definition, they all wished to be in dialogue with men, with the biblical texts, and with God about what it meant to be a woman. They were not content to submit in silence while men "named" them. The decades of the seventies and eighties have seen what might be called the beginning of the dialogue about the meaning of being female and male. And it is only a beginning. There is still much more difficult work to be done before women and men together can define and live out the fullest possible meaning of "humanity."

[38] Elsie Thomas Culver, *Women in the World of Religion* (Garden City, NY: Doubleday, 1967) 13, 202.
[39] Mary Daly, *Beyond God the Father* (Boston: Beacon, 1973) 8.

2

FEMINIST INSIGHTS
AND THE QUESTION OF METHOD

T. Drorah Setel

"Feminism" is a term that has many meanings and implications. In exploring issues related to the development of a specifically feminist methodology for biblical scholarship, this essay begins with the assumption that feminism is a distinct perspective which, although emerging from the experience of women, is applicable to human experience as a whole. As such, feminism is neither a tool for filling in the lacunae of other paradigms, unconcerned with female experience, nor is it an interest in women alone. It is possible to see feminist theories as forming the basis of a new world view, distinct from (although, of course, historically related to) those perspectives underlying predominant contemporary methodologies.

The development of feminist biblical scholarship must, therefore, begin with the very premises on which biblical studies are based. As a scholarly pursuit, contemporary biblical work supports assumptions that are reflective of the patriarchal nature of our society. Central to academic inquiry is an acceptance of the significance of "objectivity," a radical separation between the inquirer and the inquiry. This object/subject division is, however, only one portion of a comprehensive world view that perceives polarity as an essential feature of existence. In this framework, the whole context of human experience is divided into dualistic categories, such as material/spiritual; emotional/rational; night/day; death/life; passive/aggressive; bad/good; body/soul; feminine/masculine; female/male.[1]

From a feminist perspective, this dualistic perception is inextricably

---

[1] I include the biological distinction between female and male among these polarized categories because, although there are actual physiological differences between women and men, they are not so consistent or wholly separate as to necessitate the vast cultural separations that are perceived and occur between the sexes. Related to this and other insights, I would like to thank Susan T. Bruno and Martha Ackelsberg for their critical reading and discussions of my work.

linked with oppression, relating a concept of essential separateness between female and male human beings to other categorical distinctions such
as race, class, and ethnicity. Over thirty years ago, Simone de Beauvoir
articulated the connection between a dualistic mode of thought and its
implications for the dehumanizing objectification of women: "[Woman] is
defined and differentiated with reference to man and not he with reference to her; she is the incidental, the inessential as opposed to the essential.
He is the Subject, he is the Absolute—she is the Other."[2] De Beauvoir also
perceived the valuation implicit in this perspective:

> The terms *masculine* and *feminine* are used symmetrically only
> as a matter of form as on legal papers. In actuality the relation of
> the two sexes is not quite like that of two electrical poles, for man
> represents both the positive and the neutral, as is indicated by the
> common use of *man* to designate human beings in general;
> whereas woman represents only the negative, defined by limiting
> criteria, without reciprocity.[3]

Informed by an understanding of the oppressive nature of such modes
of thought, feminist scholarship cannot rest on dualistic foundations; it is
impossible to divide the process of inquiry from the formulation it produces. The pervasiveness of polarized thinking is so widespread as to make
it appear essential to human comprehension.[4] Yet, from a feminist viewpoint, to accept dualistic perception as an inevitable condition of human
experience is to accept concurrently the inevitability of oppression. More
than that, it is a means of denying responsibility for the transformation of
those beliefs and structures grounded in a polarized world view.

In her work on feminist theory, Andrea Dworkin contrasts *reality* as
a social construct, subject to change, with *truth*, which exists regardless
of any human sense of what is real. Addressing the assumption of an
innate separation between the sexes, Dworkin concludes:

---

[2] S. de Beauvoir, *The Second Sex* (Harmondsworth: Penguin Books, 1976) 15. It is
beyond the scope of this essay to summarize the fundamental arguments of feminist theory concerning the nature and implications of dualistic thought. For discussion of this
issue in a theological context see M. Daly, *Beyond God the Father* (Boston: Beacon, 1973);
and R. R. Ruether, *New Woman New Earth: Sexist Ideologies and Human Liberation*
(New York: Seabury, 1975).

[3] De Beauvoir, *The Second Sex*, 17.

[4] Claude Lévi-Strauss is an example of a theorist who sees dualistic thought as a physio-
logically, rather than socially, conditioned aspect of human existence. He argues that the
binary impulse patterns of the human nervous system dictate a basic positive/negative
polarization in human response and comprehension. See, for example, C. Lévi-Strauss,
The Raw and the Cooked (New York: Harper & Row, 1969) 1–32. Another influential
figure is, of course, Karl Marx, whose dialectical methodology is radically dualistic: despite the search for "synthesis," any resolution becomes in turn a new "thesis" in polarized
opposition to its "antithesis."

> I have made this distinction between truth and reality in order to enable me to say something very simple: *that while the system of gender polarity is real, it is not true.* It is not true that there are two sexes which are discrete and opposite, which are polar, which unite naturally and self-evidently into a harmonious whole. It is not true that the male embodies both positive and neutral human qualities and potentialities in contrast to the female. . . . In other words, the system based on this polar model of existence is absolutely real; but the model itself is not true.[5]

Using Dworkin's terminology, it is possible to differentiate between the use of dualistic categories as a means to describe aspects of historical reality and their use as a representation of truth. That is to say, distinction itself is a neutral concept inasmuch as it is a description of perceived difference which may also acknowledge similarity or relationship. In a feminist context, problems arise when distinctions are made exclusively in dualistic terms (e.g., day/night rather than day–dusk–night) and the elements of those dualisms come to be perceived as separate, and even antagonistic, descriptions of truth. In such a framework, emphasis is placed on separateness, rather than relationship. For example, the perceived phenomena of good and evil are seen as contradictory elements in need of absolute resolution, although they could be seen as a simultaneous process of relationship between points on a continuum. It is the use of dualistic categories, a concurrent stress on separation, and the failure to distinguish between reality and truth which characterize patriarchal modes of thought.

An alternative to regarding dualistic constructs as true is to see them as historical phenomena. Rosemary Ruether, for example, dates the growth of a dualistic world view from approximately 2600 Before Present,[6] when contemporary forms of religion

> . . . were born through a breakdown of the unities of tribal culture and the appearing of a way of formulating a "religious dimension" of life which split reality into distinct polarities: the sacred and the secular; the individual and the community; the soul and the body; the material and the spiritual; "this world" and the transcendent world "to come" or "above."[7]

---

[5] A. Dworkin, *Our Blood* (New York: Perigee, 1976) 110.

[6] In attempting to recover our history, feminists may wish to consider the measurement of time as an excellent example of the silencing of large portions of human experience. Rather than accept as universally applicable measurements based on the perspective of one specific group (e.g., Christians, men, Jews), it may be necessary to use different systems of dating in appropriate contexts. As we have yet to develop a concept of historical periods that takes into account the transitional points in women's experience, I choose to use the undifferentiated designation "Before Present."

[7] R. R. Ruether, *Liberation Theology* (New York: Paulist Press, 1972) 6. Naturally, the details of this process were not universal and require more research.

Such a historical understanding affirms the potential of feminist scholarship to conceive methodologies that act against oppressive modes of thought rather than being forced to utilize them.

As a paradigm emerging in its own right, feminism demands the development of an integrative means of description. This task will itself entail a long process of exploration. In attempting to articulate an alternative system of analysis feminists are discovering that there are not even terms for the concepts being envisioned. The terms *contrast* and *delineate*, for instance, have no methodological companions such as *similarize* or *unify*. In addition, because we ourselves are products of a society that thinks in polarized terms, we continue to find ourselves using its modes, sometimes only able to raise our ideas "in opposition" to what now exists. Nevertheless, there are several areas in which feminists have already begun to examine alternatives to dualistic assumptions.

If any statement can be seen as the key to a feminist perspective, it is the concept that "the personal is political." In other words, personal, individual experience is inextricably linked to the larger institutional and historical structures in which we live. In contrast to a perceived disparity among various spheres of existence (e.g., private/public, material/spiritual), feminism posits a world view that sees significance in connection and relationship rather than in contrast and separation. This perspective has crucial implications concerning the nature of knowledge and scholarship.

The difference between a perspective based on separation and one based on relationship can be tied not only to a difference in theoretical views but also to the experiential divisions between women and men in our society. Sexism has resulted in what may be termed a sexual division of human nature, that is to say, a system of socialization through which women and men acquire not just different roles but, with those experiential differences, separate ways of knowing and analyzing human experience.[8] The existence of such a division has been supported by research such as Carol Gilligan's work on moral development, which indicates that the idea and experience of separation play a much greater role in male perspectives than in female ones. In general, Gilligan found that the women she studied conceptualized and experienced reality in terms of relationship, not just as young children, dependent on adult care, but throughout their lives.[9] This consistent relational perspective can be seen as a means of understanding why and how women literally think differently from men in contemporary cultures.

In light of their developmental experience of separation, it is not

---

[8] My understanding of the sexual division of human nature developed in conversations with E. M. Ettorre. She discusses her perspective on this concept in her book *Lesbians, Women and Society* (London: Routledge & Kegan Paul, 1980) 169.

[9] C. Gilligan, *In a Different Voice: Psychological Theory and Women's Development* (Cambridge: Harvard University Press, 1982).

surprising that male scholars have produced a model of knowledge concerned with the realization of objectivity and disinterest. Constructing feminist forms of scholarship entails questioning the value and implications of working within such a model. Understanding how the actual form of academic inquiry reflects male experience makes evident the fact that the discussion of women does not in and of itself constitute a feminist perspective. There is an inevitable distortion present in the image of women seen through an essentially patriarchal lens.

Developing feminist methodology, therefore, involves considering the apparent distinctions between separation and connection, disinterest and relation, male and female perspectives in this society. It is important to bear in mind the possibility of a model in which these are not necessary or polarized divisions, again, creating a demand for new language. Positing a combination of the dualistic opposites in a "balance" or "synthesis" of existing stereotypic polarities is insufficient. Apart from the retention of those polarities, such a process rests on the extremely problematic assumption that these categories are in any way equivalent, for example, that disinterest is just the opposite of relationship and has in and of itself no greater or lesser value.

Rather than claiming a disinterest based on subject/object dualism, feminist scholarship values and seeks to articulate the personal bases of inquiry. This entails not only a statement of background but also a recognition of the goals implicit or explicit in the research; the questions we ask are not only based on past experience but also on our present concerns and expectations for the future. Learning occurs at the intersections between theory or abstract information and personal experience. In this framework, discussion that takes place solely in absolute and universal terms is not merely inadequate to the task of developing useful knowledge; it perpetuates a false description of reality—or, in Dworkin's terms, the description of a false reality.

Applying even these preliminary considerations to the field of biblical studies opens up historical and theological issues in addition to methodological ones. On a historical level, feminist biblical scholarship affirms the significance of female experience throughout human history. Dismissal of all biblical texts as completely devoid of that experience is an implicit acceptance of women's historical nonexistence. The Bible has yet to be thoroughly examined from a feminist perspective, concerned not only with women's experience but also with relating that experience to the social and political structures of patriarchy. As indicated earlier, such a perspective does not view systematic male domination as inevitable but as a historical process which can, therefore, be described and evaluated as such. Thus, the significance of feminist biblical scholarship lies not only in its recovery of women's history but also in its potential to produce an increasingly sophisticated analysis of the development of

Western patriarchy. As a compilation of materials extending over a thousand-year period, the Hebrew Bible is capable of providing important insights into the nature and causes of the expansion of patriarchal societies. It must not, however, be mistaken for a documentation of the origins of patriarchy, which preceded the biblical era.[10]

In order to develop a detailed, historical view of patriarchy it may be useful to work with a concept of "sexual structure," a model for considering the power relationship between women and men as an analytic factor comparable to political structure, economic structure, social structure, etc. A model of sexual structure can serve as a means to research and articulate a level of meaning in the biblical text which has been virtually ignored. The small amount of existing research concerned with the significance of female experience indicates, for example, that changes in sexual structure were an important factor in the determination of other communal structures in biblical society.[11] Examination of sexual structure may also lead to a reevaluation of scholarly assumptions concerning such basic issues as historical periodization and the significance of popular, in relationship to elite, experience.[12]

Feminist concern with connection and relationship also implies a historical perspective reflective of those principles. As in other areas of Western scholarship, separation and difference have served as the criteria of significance. Thus history, in general, and biblical history, in particular, are discussed as processes of "change" and "events" in a linear sequence rather than, for instance, a shifting movement in which the new is slowly interwoven with the larger fabric of older, continued experience.[13] This latter perspective is particularly important in view of the extent to which contemporary biblical scholarship focuses on the separation and difference of, for example, the Yahwists[14] from the (other) Canaanites or early Christians

---

[10] This problem is addressed by Judith Plaskow in her article "Blaming the Jews for the Birth of Patriarchy," in *Nice Jewish Girls: A Lesbian Anthology* (ed. E. T. Beck; Watertown, MA: Persephone Press, 1982) 250–54.

[11] See, for example, C. Meyers, "The Roots of Restriction: Women in Early Israel," *Biblical Archaeologist* 42 (1978) 91–103. Another example, which does not, however, deal with the issue of causality, is C. V. Camp, "The Wise Women of 2 Samuel: A Role Model for Women in Early Israel?" *Catholic Biblical Quarterly* 43 (1981) 14–29.

[12] This process has, of course, been going on for some time in other areas of historical scholarship. See, for example, J. Kelly-Gadol, "The Social Relations of the Sexes: Methodological Implications of Women's History," *Signs* 1 (1976) 809–23.

[13] I am reluctant to use the term "continuity" in this context inasmuch as it has taken on a very different meaning within deconstructionist theory. By continued experience I do not mean to imply any singular or dominant theme of historical development but rather to indicate the oversimplification and distortion involved in attempting to discern such a pattern rather than look at larger networks of interconnection.

[14] The term "Yahwist" is used here in preference to "Israelite" or "Hebrew" in describing the distinguishing characteristic of the religious culture that produced the Hebrew Bible.

from the (other) Jews of the time.

Working with an assumption of relationship not only leads to alternative interpretations of existing material; it also points to significant areas of further research. For instance, a feminist perspective on biblical history will have no difficulty in acknowledging textual and archaeological evidence that popular Yahwistic practice was similar to, if not identical with, the polytheism of all known cultures in ancient southwest Asia and northeast Africa.[15] If one does not assume separation from the beginning, the issue arises of the *process* by which Yahwistic belief and practice became differentiated from surrounding traditions. Thus, for example, in light of the fact that cultures throughout the area had female cultic functionaries, a relational method perceives the question of how and why Yahwists *excluded* women from the priesthood.

As an interpretive principle, relation also illuminates connections between historical and theological issues. This is evident in addressing textual authority and composition. Rather than positing a separation for feminists between "liberating" prophetic faith and "oppressive" laws or imagery,[16] a relational perspective specifically focuses on the fact that the very prophets who articulated such powerful visions of social justice and redemption also contributed some of the most vividly misogynistic material in the Hebrew Bible. Similarly, legal codes that regard women as the property of father or husband also display an outspoken opposition to the oppression of the poor and unprotected in society, regardless of sex. Concern with the nature and implications of these and other *relationships* allows the development of a feminist perspective which need not "cut and paste" the biblical text to value its significance. An interest in relational understanding can, in fact, be seen as demanding an extension of the text beyond the written word, placing it within a perspective inclusive of female and other non-elite experience.

At the same time, historical perspective should not be used as an excuse for continuing a separation between the form and message of biblical material. It is possible, for example, to understand the extreme misogyny of Ezekiel as the author's response to his own experience of powerlessness and humiliation. Yet it is also important to recognize and examine the fact that he used specifically female imagery and to interpret his prophecy in *relationship* to the means he chose, not as something external to it. In fact, the use of female imagery in prophetic writings

---

[15] Geographic description of the area is used here in preference to terms, such as "Near East" or "Syria-Palestine," which carry Euro-centric or political overtones. In so doing, I follow the example of R. Schiemann, "The Relevance of Archaeology to the Study of Ancient West Semitic Religion," *World Archaeology* 1/2 (1978) 129n.

[16] In addition to assuming a dualistic framework, this perspective has the unfortunate result of seeming to support anti-Jewish tendencies in Christian theology which view law as a vehicle of repression rather than revelation.

generally indicates that literary prophecy may well have been as much a response to changes in the sexual structure as in the political, social, and economic structures of the period.

Following the example of Carter Heyward's work on the significance of relation for contemporary feminist theology,[17] it is possible to apply relational considerations to biblical theology as well. In so doing, however, it is important that feminists not ignore what is perhaps the more difficult task of applying the value of relation to our own experience of the text and the history with which it is connected. We may need to remind ourselves of the nature of relationship as a process rather than a rigid establishment of authority. Arthur Waskow has described this process as one of "Godwrestling": "We do not simply accept the tradition, but we do not reject it either. We wrestle it: fighting it and making love to it at the same time. We try to touch it with our lives."[18] Such a perspective acknowledges the part of human experience in the authority of the text; it is not an external entity from which we are separate.

Similarly, as teachers, writers, and theorists, feminist biblical scholars are not merely revising the content of an established field; our work is reconceiving its form and intent as well. With other feminists we are questioning basic assumptions concerning the nature of scholarship. The broad range of issues to be addressed gives an indication of the youth and enormity of our task. Yet, it is not just the past but also the experience of our own work that can be seen as a transforming process of interconnections.

[17] I. C. Heyward, *The Redemption of God: A Theology of Mutual Relation* (Washington, DC: University Press of America, 1982).

[18] A. I. Waskow, *Godwrestling* (New York: Schocken Books, 1978) 11.

3

REMEMBERING THE PAST IN CREATING THE FUTURE: HISTORICAL-CRITICAL SCHOLARSHIP AND FEMINIST BIBLICAL INTERPRETATION

Elisabeth Schüssler Fiorenza

Recently I was involved in a discussion with students at one of the leading theological schools in this country. The women expressed their need for feminist biblical education and hermeneutics. One of them articulated their complaints well: "I have just come from this course that purports to introduce us to New Testament interpretation. But the guy talked a whole hour about historical-critical studies developed by German men in the last century. However, I am a second career student and I do not have the time and the patience to bother with questions formulated by men in the past. What I want to do is to confront my own questions with the biblical text in order to find out whether it has something to say to my questions and to see what a feminist interpretation of the Bible would do to my preaching and teaching of the Bible."

I was impressed and at the same time uneasy. I was impressed with this woman's articulate statement of her own theological goals challenging the established scholarship of the school. Remembering my own docility and "unconsciousness" as a woman student twenty years ago I realized with pride that the work of the past decade developing feminist theology and biblical interpretation has had some success in enabling women to articulate their own questions and to challenge the prevailing androcentric frameworks of scholarship. At the same time I was uneasy because the student was so certain that historical-critical scholarship had nothing to say to her own feminist theological quest and therefore easily could be discarded. I at least had experienced historical-critical scholarship as liberating, setting me free from outdated doctrinal frameworks and literalist prejudices. Was it just that nobody had bothered to make connections between her feminist theological questions and those of historical-critical scholarship? Or could it be that I experienced historical-critical scholarship as opening up intellectual doors because I was pre-feminist when I was introduced to it? Was she right in her assumption and had I just been co-opted into thinking otherwise? Or was I just naive? I had always found historical-critical method helpful for feminist critical interpretation and therefore assumed that any resistance to such an interpretation was not due to the method but due to academic bias against women and their questions. What was it then that prohibited women in biblical studies from raising their feminist questions as legitimate intellectual-historical problems? Were historical-critical methods such as textual criticism, philology, archaeology, history of religions, tradition history, form and redaction criticism at the root of the resistance to the feminist permeation of the field, or were the assumptions and frameworks of the historical-critical biblical discipline the source of the problem, and how much could method and conceptual frameworks be separated?

I. *The Rankean Understanding of History*

This quandary caused by my conversation with women students was deepened upon my return home where I found a German collection of essays on "Woman in Early Christianity."[1] The contributions were written by my fellow students with whom I had shared exegetical discussions of the Schnackenburg doctoral seminar and had many theological-critical dialogues over *Frankenwein* during my student days. The volume pretends to be a response to the emancipatory tendencies of women in the church, but in reality it is an attack on a feminist critical hermeneutics that asks not for the topical study of "Woman in the New Testament" but for a feminist reconceptualization of early Christian history that could locate women's historic role not just at the margin of social-ecclesial relations but also in the center of them. Therefore prominent scholarship, the objectivity, reliability, and the strictly historical approach of the authors are stressed. "In order to engage in a discussion appropriate to the subject matter *(sachgerecht)* an exact knowledge of the New Testament foundation is necessary. How was it in the beginning?" Established and "well-known" authors (none of them a feminist exegete!) explore the statements of the New Testament on *Woman* with *wissenschaftlicher* objectivity and scientific methods. What early Christianity has to say about the role of woman is here *zuverlassig* (reliable), presented for the discussion on the "woman question" *(Frauenthema)* in the church. An additional contribution on feminist theology was especially solicited from a woman, who, however, is not a biblical scholar

---

[1] G. Dautzenberg, H. Merklein, K. Müller (eds.), *Die Frau im Urchristentum* (Quaestiones Disputatae 95; Freiburg: Herder, 1983). The preface does not mention that the conference as well as this collection of papers was an indirect response to my paper "Der Beitrag der Frau zur urchristlichen Bewegung: Kritische Überlegungen zur Rekonstruktion urchristlicher Geschichte," in *Traditionen der Befreiung, 2: Frauen in der Bibel* (ed. W. Schottroff and W. Stegemann; Munich: Kaiser; Gelnhausen: Burckardthaus Verlag, 1980) 60–90.

and thus not an equal partner in dialogue. Nevertheless the editors insist that the objective of the volume is not a direct discussion of present-day topics or hypotheses of feminist theology but rather the collection and interpretation of all the New Testament texts on "die Frau." No mention is made, however, that several scholarly collections and interpretations of these texts are already available and that the *wissenschaftlich* hermeneutic-methodological discussion has advanced beyond such a "topical" treatment of woman[2] in the singular.

Since I am interested here not in evaluating this particular collection of essays but rather in examining its male scholarly rhetoric against a feminist critical biblical interpretation, it is necessary to look at the understanding of historical-critical method and its goals as presented there. Again I am interested not in evaluating this particular volume but in using it as a "case study" to pinpoint the source of tension between historical-critical and feminist-historical biblical studies. The *antiquarian* understanding of historical-critical studies as it was formulated in the last century by Ranke comes to the fore in the introduction to the article on the household code of Colossians. This statement is quoted at length because it indicates the emotions and interests that inspire the rhetoric of scientific, reliable, and well-established historical-critical scholarship that claims not to be influenced by present-day concerns.

> Von den derzeit für ihre Rechte in der Gesellschaft immer heftiger rebellierenden Frauen werden mit Vorzug die sogenannten "Haustafeln" des Neuen Testaments ins Spiel gebracht, wenn sie ihre gewöhnlich harsche und resignierte Abrechnung mit den Überlieferungen und den Institutionen eines Christentums vortragen, das nach ihrer Auffassung nicht unerheblich die Unterdrückung der Frauen gefördert und stabilisiert hat. . . .
>   Es ist also keine Frage: in einem Buch über "Die Frau im Urchristentum" müssen die "Haustafeln" ein wichtiges Thema sein. Dabei ist es allerdings nützlich, gleich eingangs die Grenzen zu markieren, an die der Neutestamentler gehalten bleiben muss, wenn er seine methodische Glaubwürdigkeit nicht verspielen will.
>   Er darf nämlich seine berufliche Ehre nur darin finden, jene antiken Texte eben *nicht* in das Geflecht moderner emanzipatorischer Regungen und Gewissheiten zu verspannen, sondern sie korrelational zu ihrer Entstehungszeit am Ausgang des ersten

---

[2] See especially J. Neusner, *Method and Meaning in Ancient Judaism* (Brown Judaic Studies 10; Missoula, MT: Scholars Press, 1979); A. Carroll, ed., *Liberating Women's History: Theoretical and Critical Essays* (Urbana: University of Illinois Press, 1976); J. Kelly-Gadol, "The Social Relations of the Sexes: Methodological Implications of Women's History," *Signs* 1 (1976) 809–23; J. Lewis, "Women Lost and Found: The Impact of Feminism on History," in *Men's Studies Modified: The Impact of Feminism on the Academic Disciplines* (ed. D. Spender; Oxford and New York: Pergamon Press, 1981) 73–82; and my own book *In Memory of Her: A Feminist Theological Reconstruction of Christian Origins* (New York: Crossroad, 1983) 3–95.

Jahrhunderts nach Christus verständlich zu machen. Das aber heisst vor allem: er kann ihre objektive ethische Qualität nur aus dem Vergleich mit mehr oder weniger vagen Durchschnitts- margen für soziales Verhalten in der späthellenistischen Antike erkennen. Er muss sich deshalb besonders davor hüten, das, was ihn heute stört, allzu flugs als damals zeitbedingt wegzuarbeiten. Seine vordringliche Aufgabe wird es vielmehr sein, gerade die anstössige *Fremdheit* jener alten Äusserungen vor dem aufgeklär- ten hermeneutischen Horizont der eigenen Gegenwart zur Gel- tung zu bringen.[3]

Such a rhetorical statement not only veils its apologetic aggressive- ness by proclaiming for itself historical objectivity, but it also advocates a nineteenth-century concept of history, based on the assumption that the historian can "step out of his own time" and study history "on its own terms," unencumbered by questions and experiences of "his own day." I deliberately use here the pronoun "he" for the historian, since women who have entered the field in the past hundred years or so could not do so on their own terms but only by adopting an androcentric conceptual framework and perspective that acknowledged women's experiences and intellectual questions only peripherally or not at all.[4] Women scholars, therefore, no less than their colleagues subscribed to the Rankean defini- tion of history as "what actually happened." To bring their own issues to their intellectual work would have meant to destroy the agreed-upon basis of this work. The feminist study of the Bible, therefore, did not originate with historical or biblical scholars in the academy but with women articulating their own biblical questions in their confrontation with antifeminist biblical arguments used against them in their struggle for liberation.[5]

The true exegete is expected to examine all the material in a truly dispassionate manner in order to study the past "for its own sake" and to find out "what actually happened." This ethos of historical-critical stud- ies is also expressed in the following statement of the British scholar I. H. Marshall, which appeared in a book on New Testament methods of interpretation:

> By "historical criticism" is meant the study of any narrative which purports to convey historical information in order to actu- ally determine what actually happened. . . . The phrase "what

---

[3] Karlheinz Müller, "Die Haustafel des Kolosserbriefes und das antike Frauenthema. Eine kritische Ruckschau auf alte Ergebnisse," in *Die Frau im Urchristentum*, 263–65.

[4] See Nancy Schrom Dye, "Clio's American Daughters: Male History, Female Reality," in *The Prism of Sex: Essays in the Sociology of Knowledge* (ed. J. A. Sherman and E. T. Beck; Madison: University of Wisconsin Press, 1979) 9–31.

[5] D. C. Bass, "Women's Studies and Biblical Studies: An Historical Perspective," *Journal for the Study of the Old Testament* 22 (1982) 6–12.

actually happened" is by no means free from difficulties of interpretation, but a common-sense view of it will suffice us in the
present discussion.[6]

The task of the historical exegete is therefore to interrogate the texts "in
order to construct a picture of the event which they reflect, a picture
which will be in itself historically coherent and which will also serve to
explain the wording of the sources."[7] If it is assumed that the New Testament texts mirror the reality of early Christian women and give us an
accurate picture of their involvement in early Christianity, then it is the
"scientific" exegete who establishes objectively "wie es am Anfang war."
Moreover, since Wilhelm Dilthey, the historian is also asked to enter
"sympathetically" into the minds of or consciousness of historical persons
to empathize with their motivations, intentions, and actions, seeing them
from their own point of view and not from that of the inquiring historian. It belongs to historical "objectivity" that interpreters seek to put
themselves into the place of historical agents whose "historicity" consists
in the fact that their values, actions, and motivations are alien—if not
strange—to the contemporary inquirer.[8]

It seems no rapprochement is possible between a feminist historical-
critical and a positivist-historical understanding. Insofar as such an
understanding of biblical historiography prides itself on being impartial,
value-neutral, objective-descriptive, scientific-antiquarian, it must reject
any feminist reconstruction of early Christian history as "ideological"
and as "influenced" by present-day concerns. A feminist-critical interpretation in turn cannot acknowledge as valid the claims and assumptions
made by such biblical scholars, if it does not want to relinquish its own
interest in the past and its own heritage. While such a value-neutral,
descriptive historical-critical scholarship can "collect" the passages on
Woman it cannot conceive of women as involved in early Christianity
equally with men. It cannot do so because it understands its androcentric
sources as "data" and its own androcentric language and narrative as
totally divorced from contemporary concerns. It overlooks thereby what
Rudolf Bultmann already had insisted on: that no understanding is possible without preunderstanding. Such scholarship claiming to be "objective" and "realistic" is not more value-free and less ideological because it

[6] I. H. Marshall, "Historical Criticism," in *New Testament Interpretation: Essays on Principles and Methods* (ed. I. H. Marshall; Grand Rapids: Eerdmans, 1977) 126.

[7] Ibid., 127; see also E. Krentz, *The Historical-Critical Method* (Philadelphia: Fortress, 1975) esp. 33–41 with bibliography.

[8] I. O. Mink, *Mind, History, and Dialectic: The Philosophy of R. G. Collingwood* (Bloomington: University of Indiana Press, 1969) 162–94; and M. Earmarth, *Wilhelm Dilthey: The Critique of Historical Reason* (Chicago: University of Chicago Press, 1978) 95–108.

hides its "subjectivity," "cultureboundedness," and "contemporary interests" from itself. Such a Rankean[9] definition of historical-critical biblical
scholarship overlooks not only the hermeneutical-critical insights of the
past one hundred years and neglects recent methodological discussions in
New Testament scholarship;[10] it also disregards the epistemological
debate among philosophers of history on the possibility and the specific
character of historical knowledge.

II. *The Historical Character of Historical Knowledge*

The debate between the "objectivist-realist" and the "constructionist"
direction in historical scholarship highlights two different perceptions of
what we can know historically.[11] The "objectivist" direction holds the
Rankean view that the past can be known scientifically and objectively.
Historical facticity and theological truth can become identical. Historians assemble historical facts, drawn from historical sources and evidence.
They use this collected evidence in order to discover and tell us what
actually happened at a certain time and certain place. At least sometimes historians succeed in describing with "scientific objectivity" the
actual events of the past.

The "constructionist" epistemology of historical knowledge stresses
its "time-boundedness" and "linguisticality," which make it impossible
for us to know the "real past" as we would know an object in the present.
Neither the description of "data" nor the establishment of "historical
facts" is scientifically verifiable, because the description of historical data
and facts is "narrative-laden." Statements of "historical fact" do not
emerge of themselves as ready-made mirrors of past events. In order to
make statements of historical fact scholars have to make inferences based
in part upon their "data" or "sources" and based in part upon their general understanding of human behavior and the nature of the world.

[9] The famous expression "wie es eigentlich gewesen" occurs in the preface, dated October 1824, to Ranke's *Geschichte der romanischen und germanischen Völker von 1494 bis
1535.* Cf. Leopold von Ranke, *The Theory and Practice of History* (ed. G. Iggers and
K. V. Moltke; Indianapolis, IN: Bobbs-Merrill, 1973) 137. The words have been translated
in various ways as "what really happened," "how it really was," or "how, essentially,
things happened."
[10] See W. G. Doty, *Contemporary New Testament Interpretation* (Englewood Cliffs,
NJ: Prentice-Hall, 1972). Especially for the challenge of literary biblical criticism to
historical-biblical criticism, see *Orientation by Disorientation. Festschrift W. A. Beards-
lee* (ed. R. A. Spencer; Pittsburgh Theological Monograph Series 35; Pittsburgh: Pickwick,
1980).
[11] See the exchange between P. H. Nowell-Smith, "The Constructionist Theory of History," and L. J. Goldstein, "History and the Primacy of Knowing," in *History and Theory:
The Constitution of the Historical Past* 16 (1977) 1–52 with literature. See also S. Bann,
"Towards a Critical Historiography: Recent Work in Philosophy of History," *Philosophy*
56 (1981) 365–85.

They not only deal selectively with their historical sources in order to present a "coherent" narrative account but also ascribe historical "significance" to their "data" in accordance with the theoretical model or perspective that "orders" their information.[12] This emphasis corresponds to insights of the hermeneutical discussion stressing that the interpreter is not able to step outside the "hermeneutical circle."

In *History and Social Theory*, Gordon Leff repeatedly states the criteria for a "good history." According to him historical "objectivity" consists not in "pure" facts or "data" but in the dynamic interrelation between the information gleaned from the sources and the "unifying vision" of the interpreter. Historians gather all available evidence, account for its correct use, and order it within a framework of reasoning. Nevertheless, historians argue from evidence as opposed to events accessible to our experience. In the attempt "to make the past intelligible" the historian must go beyond the events in an act of "intellectual recreation."[13] In doing so the historian shows at once why, for example, "Caesar's crossing of the Rubicon was significant for posterity and what it meant for Caesar and his contemporaries." In order to do so the historian must have a theoretical frame of reference and must construct a model that is at once a comparative and an ideal construct.

> The letters on a stone or a piece of parchment or the remains of a medieval village or a treatise by a schoolman, do not of themselves provide more than the data on which the historian sets to work; and in order to make them into historical facts, i.e. what he [sic] assumes to have been the case—he [sic] has to employ a full critical and interpretative apparatus of selection, evaluation, interpolation and rejection—which rests upon inference as opposed to observation, and hence can never pass beyond a high degree of probability.[14]

The relationship between thought in the present and statements about the past is constituted by the explanatory models or ideal-typical constructs that help us to organize our knowledge of the past and give meaning to it. Such explanatory models can be either *structural* models, which are static in nature and focus on the dominant elements of a given social formation, for example, feudalism, fascism, Renaissance; or they can be *developmental* models, which provide a structural-temporal line for narrative presentation. Such models can be chosen consciously or they can remain unconscious; they can be used in isolation or in combination with one another.

---

[12] See R. Stephen Humphreys, "The Historian, His Documents, and the Elementary Modes of Historical Thought," *History and Theory* 19 (1980) 1–20.
[13] G. Leff, *History and Social Theory* (Garden City, NY: Doubleday, 1971) 111.
[14] Ibid., 14.

Reconstructive inferences, selection of "data," and ascription of historical significance do not depend only on the choice of explanatory models but also on the rhetorical aims of the work. Hayden White has pointed out that historians "shape" their material not just in accordance with a narrative framework of preconceived ideas but also in response to the narrative discourse in general, which is *rhetorical* in nature.[15] In the very language historians use to describe their projects they not only provide a certain amount of explanation or interpretation of what this information *means* but also give a more or less overt message about the attitude that the reader should take with respect to the historical "data" and their interpretation. White agrees with Claude Lévi-Strauss that history is never just history *of* but always also history *for*. It is *history for* not only in the sense of being told with some ideological goal in mind but also in the sense of being written *for* a certain group of people. "The clue to the meaning of a given historical discourse is contained as much in the *rhetoric* of the description of the field as in the *logic* of whatever argument is offered."[16] Therefore, the traditional distinction between "historical facts" (data) on the one hand and their interpretation (or story told about the facts) on the other hand is misleading. It obscures the epistemological difficulty of distinguishing between these two levels.

Historical discourse itself is the actual "combination of facts and meaning which gives to it the aspect of a *specific* structure of meaning that permits us to identify it as a product of one kind of historical consciousness rather than another."[17] Thus, two levels of historical discourse can be distinguished: the "surface" level of the discourse, which consists of the historical facts *and* their interpretation; and the "generic story type" or conceptual model, to which the events are to be likened but which is not always consciously chosen. This "generic story type" can be detected in the rhetorical "clues" and "emotion-laden" words pointing to the figurative element of the discourse.

Insofar as every account of the past is mediated by the language mode in which historians describe the historical field, a nonrelativistic account of historical reality is not possible. Rankean "realism" also was "relativistic" insofar as it required that historians view the past on "its own terms" or "for

---

[15] See Hayden White, *Metahistory: The Historical Imagination in Nineteenth-Century Europe* (Baltimore: Johns Hopkins University Press, 1973); idem, *Tropics of Discourse: Essays in Cultural Criticism* (Baltimore: Johns Hopkins University Press, 1978); idem, "The Value of Narrativity in the Representation of Reality," *Critical Inquiry* 7 (1980) 5–28; idem, "The Politics of Historical Interpretation: Discipline and De-Sublimation," in *The Politics of Interpretation* (ed. W. J. T. Mitchell; Chicago: University of Chicago Press, 1983) 119–43.

[16] Hayden White, "Historicism, History, and the Figurative Imagination," *History and Theory: Essays on Historicism* 14 (1975) 54.

[17] Ibid., 55.

its own sake." Objectivity meant to think one's way back into the consciousness of the historical epoch and to get "outside" of one's own time and
culture, viewing, for example, the world of antiquity "from its own perspective" as ancient peoples would have understood it. Therefore, the
historical-critical exegete had first to find out what the text of the New
Testament *meant* in its historical context, and the preacher's task was to
"apply" it and to explicate what it *means* today.[18] Such a division, however, not only overlooks that we know "more" about the Greco-Roman
world than the early Christian might have known. It also neglects the hermeneutical insight that a "stepping outside" of one's own time and culture
is not only impossible but also undesirable. History is not written today for
people of past times but for people of our own times. The antiquarian
understanding of history is not only epistemologically impossible but also
historically undesirable. What needs to be rediscovered is the understanding of history not as artifact but as "historical consciousness" for the present
and the future, a historical consciousness that understands historical knowledge in terms of the topos coined by Cicero: *Historia magistra vitae* (*De
Oratore libri tres* 2.36).[19]

Historical knowledge is not only *history for* but also *dependent* on
the self-image of the social group for which historians speak and to
which they belong. Far from recording "what actually happened" with
the utmost objectivity and value-neutrality, historians have written history for the dominant groups in society. History was conceived as a history of empires and wars or as the history of political or cultural heroes,
and it was written in order to instill national pride or cultural hegemony.
History was made and written by the "winners"; the oppressed and
vanquished of the past do not have a "written" history.

Social historians have pointed out that we know only little about the
everyday lives of most societal groups of ordinary people. Our sources
speak only rarely about the experiences and contributions of slaves, serfs,
prostitutes, working-class people, or colonialized peoples. American historians have shown that historiography in this country was from its inception
occupied with questions of public policy and sought to imbue Americans
with a sense of national pride. "From the days of the first doctoral program
at Johns Hopkins, where 'History is past politics' was a slogan inscribed on
the seminar room wall, historians have defined their subject as a record of

---

[18] For this influential distinction in New Testament studies see especially K. Stendahl,
"Biblical Theology, Contemporary," in *The Interpreters Dictionary of the Bible* (Nash-
ville: Abingdon, 1962) 1. 418–32 and my forthcoming article "Contemporary Biblical
Scholarship: Its Roots, Present Understandings, and Future Dimensions," in *Modern Biblical Scholarship: Its Impact on Theology and Proclamation* (ed. F. A. Eigo; Villanova, PA:
Villanova University Press, 1984).
[19] Cf. T. Schieder, "The Role of Historical Consciousness in Political Action," *History
and Theory: Historical Consciousness and Political Action* 17 (1978) 3–4.

the public and political aspects of the American past."[20] Feminist historians in turn have pointed out that most histories were written as if women did not exist or as if we were some rare and exceptional creatures on the fringes of American social life.

Intellectual historians, moreover, have shown that the three eminent historians of "realist historiography," Leopold von Ranke, Friedrich Meinecke, and Benedetto Croce, were antiprogressive and politically reactionary. Ranke developed his notion of history in opposition to the Revolution of 1830 and for the sake of the Prussian governmental and social elites. Although he stated "his historical urge to survey the whole (of modern history) from a detached viewpoint" he maintained that the separation and independent development of the European states which were fortified by the centrifugal force "of the national principle" express "'the secret of world history' and thus serve as the conservative general counterpart to the 'general movement of democracy' which would dominate or homogenize the individual states."[21] In Meinecke as well as Croce realist historicism is also intertwined with clearly conservative positions. "In Meinecke it is tied to a nineteenth century conception of the national state of romantic inspiration on the one hand and Bismarckian politics on the other hand; in Croce it is intertwined with a form of liberalism which is not only ademocratic but clearly anti-democratic."[22] Thus, historical discourse is not only "narrative laden" but also intrinsically linked to the specific social-political reality in which it arises and to the social-political location of the historian who produces it.

The past is not a continuum of given facts that we can rediscover by mere objective observation, but it discloses itself to us only if we put specific questions to it. We historians never are able to free ourselves totally from our own experiential presuppositions or institutional interests, and we should not even attempt to do so. What makes our work interesting and fruitful are exactly the specific questions, concerns, insights, perspectives, and commitments that compel us to study a certain epoch of the past or to choose from the complexity of historical reality those elements that enable us to make the causal link between the past and our world. Therefore all historical discourse and judgment stand

> as it were with one foot rooted in the self-image of a certain group in society. The current values, interests, and traditions of the group to which the historian belongs and which makes up his [sic] audience determine not only the subject matter the historian examines and perspective he [sic] brings to bear on it but also the explanatory models he [sic] uses to conceptualize and explain the

[20] N. Schrom Dye, "Clio's American Daughters," 9.
[21] L. Krieger, "Elements of Early Historicism: Experience, Theory and History in Ranke," *History and Theory: Essays on Historicism* 14 (1975) 8–9.
[22] P. Rossi, "The Ideological Valences of Twentieth-Century Historicism," 23.

multifarious historical phenomena before him [sic]. This is precisely what provides historical judgments with the meaning and
relevance they have for a reader who is confronted by them as a
human being whose interests are primarily determined by the
intellectual context of the present.[23]

Not value-neutrality but public consciousness and discussions of one's
values, interests, commitments, presuppositions, and social-political location are required for historical discourse.[24] The self-conscious relativity
and multiformity of historical inquiry create conditions for maximum
communication across ideological lines. Nevertheless historical narrative
and judgments are not totally relativistic and can be distinguished from
mere fictive accounts. They are open to and necessarily subject to scholarly scrutiny. They can be tested in terms of the source material they
draw on and in terms of the assumptions and models underlying them.
In other words, historical judgments are intersubjectively understandable
and intersubjectively verifiable. The following criteria for publicly testing historical knowledge are proposed: (1) To what extent have relevant
sources been utilized and how much has the present state of research
been considered? (2) How much has the account reached an optimal
plausible integration of all available historical information? (3) How
logically rigorous, consistent and coherent are the explanatory heuristic
models used, and are they reasonably free from self-contradictions?
Explanatory models must be "adequate" to the historical object under
consideration.[25]

Such public discussion of historical constructions as *history for* can
be a valuable aid for clarifying the self-understanding of social groups as
active participants in history. Liberation theology has therefore insisted
that historical-critical biblical scholarship begin with an analysis of its
own historical-political situation and with the articulation of one's "hermeneutical preference" rather than with the pretension of "objective"
"truly historical" scholarship. This demand is in accordance with historical thinking, for

> the social value that history as a discipline provides lies in sub-
> jecting prevalent historical assumptions to rational analysis, thereby

[23] W. J. Mommsen, "Social Conditioning and Social Relevance of Historical Judgments,"
History and Theory: Historical Consciousness and Political Action 17 (1978) 32.

[24] See also D. H. Porter (*The Emergence of the Past: A Theory of Historical Explanation* [Chicago: University of Chicago Press, 1981]), who ends with the hope that "if the
approach to explanation outlined in this book is found useful, more and more historians
will preface their narrative accounts with explanations of their theoretical and methodological presuppositions. Also philosophers of history will relate their analytic arguments
more directly to actual examples of historical writing. In this way, communication can
increase within a framework that grows gradually more intelligible to both sides" (p. 179).

[25] W. J. Mommsen, "Social Conditioning and Social Relevance," 33.

> testing for validity the understanding that social groups have of
> themselves. Historical thought is valuable not only as an anti-
> dogmatic weapon . . . but also as a critical and rational instrument
> of inquiring into the historical dimensions of contemporary value
> systems and of self-understanding of contemporary societies.[26]

Such public historical discourse not only among historians but also
among biblical interpreters and theologians would reduce the danger
that communications will be broken off either with one's own tradition
or with the traditions of different cultures, religions, and times. Finally,
such public historical discourse can create the possibility for stepping
"somewhat" outside our present horizons, insofar as it allows us to
remain conscious of our human and historical relativity and potential.
Studying the past for recovering its unfulfilled historical possibilities
becomes a primary task for historical inquiry.[27] It enables us to keep our
future "open" in the light of our historical heritage and identity.

In conclusion, I have attempted to show that a certain reified understanding of history is contrary to feminist interests, insofar as it is exclusive of women's questions and thus of women as historical subjects. The
truly historical understanding of historical inquiry, on the contrary,
invites active feminist participation in the writing of human history in
order to keep "open" our unfulfilled historical possibilities for a more
human future. Moreover, I would maintain that such an understanding
of historical inquiry is not open just to feminist participation but is more
appropriate also to biblical interpretation. It enables us to see the Bible
not just as a history of Israel or the ministry of Jesus and the early
church but also as history *for* certain communities and people. It allows
us to integrate biblical history and biblical theology as historical rhetoric
for believing communities.[28] It allows for a feminist-critical interpretation of the Bible as a historical rhetoric for women-church.

Rapprochement between feminist biblical and academic biblical
scholarship is possible only in contexts in which biblical-historical scholarship has taken cognizance of the new developments in historical epistemology and critical hermeneutics and is *willing* to shed its outdated
assumptions of "scientific factuality" and pretensions of "positivist objectivity," as well as honestly to articulate its own social-ecclesial-political

---

[26] Ibid., 34.
[27] This aspect is stressed by P. Hernadi ("Clio's Cousins: Historiography as Translation,
Fiction, and Criticism," *New Literary History* 7 [1975/76] 248), who with Friedrich
Schlegel argues that the historian always also must be "a prophet turned backward" who
must discern in the past "what shall be remembered."
[28] See J. Barr, "The Bible as a Document of Believing Communities," in *The Bible as a
Document of the University* (ed. H. D. Betz; Chico, CA: Scholars Press, 1981) 25–47. See
also my "For the Sake of Our Salvation: Biblical Interpretation as Theological Task," *Sin,
Salvation, and the Spirit* (ed. D. Durken; Collegeville, MN: Liturgical Press, 1979) 21–39.

locations and interests.[29] In short, such rapprochement is possible only when established biblical scholarship recognizes its male-centeredness as a scholarly-intellectual "handicap" and in a process of public consciousness-raising has the chance to become truly "historical consciousness."

III. *Historical-Critical Feminist Interpretation*

Although women have participated in the production and teaching of historical-critical scholarship for more than a hundred years, it is for the first time that we now seek consciously to do such scholarship and biblical interpretation not just for the academy or the"church" but for all women affected by biblical religion, and especially for women-church.[30] In order to do so, I would argue, we need to use the methods and means of historical inquiry developed by historical-critical scholarship while at the same time scrutinizing and contesting its androcentric philosophical-theological presuppositions, perspectives, and goals.

Feminist studies as an intellectual discipline has only begun to articulate the challenge that such a shift in commitment and scholarly goal of inquiry implies for historical knowledge and for a truly human historical consciousness. Feminist scholars in all areas of intellectual inquiry are in the process of inaugurating a scientific revolution that engenders a paradigm shift from an androcentric—male-centered—world view and intellectual framework of discourse to a feminist comprehension of the world, human culture, and history.[31] While androcentric scholarship takes *man* as the paradigmatic subject of scientific knowledge and defines women as the "other," or the object of male scholarship, feminist scholarship insists on the reconceptualization of our language as well as of our intellectual frameworks so that women as well as men become the

---

[29] See especially F. Herzog, "Liberation Hermeneutics as Ideology Critique," *Interpretation* 27 (1974) 387–403; J. L. Segundo, *The Liberation of Theology* (Maryknoll, NY: Orbis Books, 1976); L. Cormee, "The Hermeneutical Privilege of the Oppressed: Liberation Theologies, Biblical Faith and Marxist Sociology of Knowledge," *Proceedings of the Catholic Theological Society of America* 32 (1978) 155–81.

[30] See my "Toward a Feminist Biblical Hermeneutics: Biblical Interpretation and Liberation Theology," in *The Challenge of Liberation Theology: A First World Response* (ed. B. Mahan and D. Richesin; Maryknoll, NY: Orbis Books, 1981) 91–112 and my forthcoming "For the Sake of the Truth Dwelling Among Us: Emerging Issues in Feminist Biblical Interpretation," in *Visions of a New Humanity* (ed. Judith Weidman; New York: Harper & Row, 1984).

[31] *Signs: Journal of Women in Culture and Society*, which was founded in 1975, has regular review articles of feminist scholarship in various disciplines. For most recent collections of essays on such an intellectual paradigm shift, see *Discovering Reality: Feminist Perspectives on Epistemology, Metaphysics, Methodology, and Philosophy of Science* (ed. S. Harding and M. B. Hintikka; Synthese Libr. 161; Boston: D. Reidel, 1983) and *Feminismus: Inspektion der Herrenkultur* (ed. L. F. Pusch; Edition Suhrkamp NF 192; Frankfurt: Suhrkamp, 1983).

subjects of intellectual inquiry.

Such a shift from an androcentric to a feminist construction of the world and of history not only challenges the established intellectual frameworks of male scholarship but also questions their claim to objectivity and value-neutrality.

> But insisting that women be entered into sociology [or history] as its subjects, we find that we cannot escape how its practices transform us into objects. As women we become objects to ourselves as subjects. . . . So long as "men," "he," and "his" appeared as the general and impersonal terms locating the subject of sociological assertions, the problem remained invisible. We had learned to "enter" our subjectivities into sentences beginning "he" and to disattend our sex under the convention—applying only to women since it is irrelevant for men—that the pronoun was in this context neutral. Once we had understood, however, that the male pronoun did indeed locate a male subject for whom women were constituted in the sociological relation outside the frame which organized his position, the appearance of impersonality went. The knower turns out after all not to be "abstract knower" perching on an Archimedian point but a member of a definite social category occupying definite positions in the society.[32]

Feminist studies therefore maintains that established scholarship as androcentric scholarship is not only *partial* insofar as it articulates only male experience as human experience, but that it is also *biased* insofar as its intellectual discourse and scholarly frameworks are determined only by male perspectives primarily of the dominant classes. This feminist claim runs counter to the rhetoric of traditional historical-critical biblical scholarship, which prides itself on being impartial, objective, and value-neutral. Recognizing its social-political location and public commitment, a feminist biblical interpretation, therefore, must utilize historical-critical methods for the sake of presenting an alternative interpretation of biblical texts and history to public scholarly discussion and historical assessment. In order to be able to do so, it must develop a "hermeneutics of suspicion," which needs to be applied not just to the contemporary scholarly historical discourse but also to that of the biblical writers. Such a feminist "hermeneutics of suspicion" understands androcentric texts as selective articulations of men often expressing as well as maintaining patriarchal historical conditions.

As androcentric texts our early Christian sources are theological interpretations, argumentations, projections, and selections rooted in a patriarchal culture. Therefore they need to be read critically for their theoretical-theological androcentric tendencies and their polemical theological patriarchal functions. Such texts must be evaluated *historically* in

[32] Dorothy E. Smith, "A Sociology for Women," in *The Prism of Sex*, 159–60.

terms of their own time and culture and assessed *theologically* in terms of a feminist scale of values. A careful analysis of their androcentric tendencies and patriarchal functions, nevertheless, can provide clues for constructing a historical model of interpretation that does justice to the egalitarian as well as the patriarchalizing tendencies and developments in the early church. The critical analysis of androcentric biblical texts needs to be utilized positively for a feminist reconstruction of Christian origins in order to arrive at a feminist biblical consciousness. A "hermeneutics of suspicion" must lead to a feminist "hermeneutics of remembrance."

In the past decade women historians have articulated the theoretical problem of how to move from androcentric text to historical context and of how to write women into history. Scholars of American history in particular have pointed out that the task of feminist historical interpretation is the placing of the lives of all women at the center of historical reconstructions as women's responses to social changes affecting their lives as well as at the center of women's efforts to transform and change societal structures and institutions.

> Feminist historians are asking what it was like to be a woman at various times in history and are exploring women's subjective responses to their environment. . . . In short, new approaches to women's history are attempting to integrate women into the mainstream of American historical development rather than isolating woman as a separate category.[33]

Historians, therefore, point out that the literature on women in history is too often limited by narrowly focusing on woman as a topical or heuristic category rather than exploring new conceptual frameworks that would allow us to place women at the center of human social relations and political institutions. Feminist historians, furthermore, question the androcentric scholarly evaluation of "historical significance" as well as point out that many of the historical sources on women are not descriptive but prescriptive. Women are neglected in the writing of history, although the effects of their lives and actions are a reality in history. Ideas of men *about* women, therefore, do not reflect women's historical reality since it can be shown that ideological polemics about women's place, role, or nature increase whenever women's actual emancipation and active participation in history become stronger.

Some feminist historians, therefore, propose a theoretical framework that can maintain the dialectical tension of women's historical existence, namely, to be at one and the same time active participants in history as well as objects of patriarchal oppression. Since gender dimorphism is

[33] A. D. Gordon, M. J. Buhle, N. Schrom Dye, "The Problem of Women's History," *Liberating Women's History* (ed. B. A. Carroll; Urbana: University of Illinois Press, 1976) 8.

generated by such patriarchal oppression, it is not "natural" but social.[34] Therefore we must reject heuristic concepts such as "biological-caste" or "women's experience" as essentially different from that of men, because these categories render women as passive objects of biological differences or of male dominance.

We must seek instead heuristic models that explore women's historical participation in social-public development and their efforts to comprehend and transform social structures. It is not "biological" sex difference but patriarchal household and marriage relationships that generate the social-political inferiority and oppression of women. Patriarchy is at home in the patriarchal household and its property relationships rather than in innate biological differences between women and men.[35] Wherever the "private sphere" of the patriarchal house is sharply delineated from that of the public order of the state, women are more dependent and exploited, whereas in those societies in which the boundaries between the household and the public domain are not so sharply drawn, women's positions and roles are more equal to those of men. While the public sphere is stratified by class differences, the domestic patriarchal sphere is determined by sexual role differences and dependencies.

Whereas some scholars of women's history and religion have postulated matriarchy as an oppositional structure to patriarchy, others have constructed heuristic models that can help us to measure women's power and influence within patriarchal history. In order to do so they seek not only to restore women to history and history to women but also to reconceptualize history and culture as the product and experience of both women and men. Women's experience of solidarity and unity as a social group is not based on their biological differences from men but on their common historical experiences as an oppressed group struggling to become full historical subjects. Such a theoretical framework allows women to locate their strength, historical agency, pain, and struggle within their common historical experiences as women in patriarchal society and family. It is also theoretically able to account for the variations of social status, class differences, and cultural identity.

Such a feminist theoretical framework encompasses a "view of

[34] See especially H. Smith, "Feminism and the Methodology of Women's History," in *Liberating Women's History*, 369–84; M. Zimbalist Rosaldo, "The Use and Abuses of Anthropology: Reflections on Feminism and Cross-Cultural Understandings," *Signs* 5 (1980) 400–402; and my forthcoming "Claiming the Center: A Critical Feminist Theology of Liberation," in *Womenspirit Bonding* (New York: Pilgrim Press, 1984).

[35] This classical understanding of patriarchy was developed by Aristotle and is still operative in Western culture. See S. Moller Okin, *Women in Western Political Thought* (Princeton: University Press, 1979); and my "Discipleship and Patriarchy: Early Christian Ethos and Christian Ethics in a Feminist Theological Perspective," in *The Annual of the Society of Christian Ethics 1982* (ed. L. Rasmussen; Waterloo, Ont.: CSR, 1982) 131–72.

women's historic role as located simultaneously in the center of social relations and at the edge of them." It thereby allows us to explore patriarchy as the source of women's oppression as well as of women's power. Such an interest of women in their own social history is very much like colonialized peoples' interest in unearthing their own past.

> The search to understand collective conditions and the relations of race to the dominant society has enabled blacks to locate their strengths, their social importance, and the sources of their oppression. Furthermore, this process has provided an analytical framework for recognizing their unity through historical experience, rather than simply through their racial difference from the ruling caste.[36]

Like historians of other oppressed groups and peoples, feminist historians, therefore, seek to honeycomb androcentric records for feminist meaning by reappropriating the patriarchal past for those who have suffered not only its pain of oppression but also participated in its social transformation and development. As biblical historians we can do so because the canonization process of early Christian writings has preserved not only the patriarchalizing texts of the New Testament but also those earliest Christian traditions and texts that still permit us a glimpse of the egalitarian-inclusive practice and theology of early Christians. These texts are like the tip of an iceberg indicating a possibly rich heritage now lost to us. Therefore we must cease interpreting the women's passages in the New Testament in isolation from their historical-ecclesial-social contexts. What is necessary is a systemic interpretation and historical reconstruction that can make the submerged bulk of the iceberg "visible."[37]

The scant references to women as well as the inconsistencies in our New Testament sources indicate not only that women were members and leaders in the early Christian movement but also that the early Christian traditioning and redactional processes followed certain androcentric interests and theological perspectives. This androcentric selection and transmission of early Christian traditions seems to have engendered the historical marginality of women. New Testament texts are not an accurate reflection of the historical reality of women's leadership and participation in the early Christian movement.

It is important to note that the redaction of the gospels and of Acts happened at a time when the patriarchalization process of the early church was well under way. Since for various reasons the New Testament authors were not interested in extolling women's and slaves' active participation in

---

[36] A. D. Gordon, M. J. Buhle, N. Schrom Dye, "The Problem of Women's History," 85.

[37] See my book *In Memory of Her*, especially chapters IV–VIII, for an attempt at such a historical reconstruction.

the Christian movement, we can methodologically assume that the early Christian writers transmit only a fraction of the possibly rich traditions of women's contributions to the early Christian movement.[38] Much of the information and traditions about the agency of women in the beginnings of Christianity are irretrievable because the patriarchal transmission and redaction process considered these stories and information either as insignificant or as a threat to the gradual patriarchalization of the Christian movement. A feminist reading of biblical texts and the reconstructions of their historical-social worlds need therefore to utilize all the available historical-critical methods and means of inquiry, in order to reconstruct the historical-theological tendencies and rhetorical aims of the redactional as well as of the history of tradition processes.

If the "silences" about women's historical experience and theological contributions in the early Christian movement are produced by androcentric language, texts, and historical models of reconstruction, then we have to find ways to "break" the silences of the texts and to derive meaning from androcentric historiography and narrative. Rather than understand the texts as an adequate reflection of the reality about which they speak, we have to search for rhetorical clues and allusions that indicate the reality about which the texts are silent. Rather than take androcentric biblical texts as informative "data" and objective reports, we have to understand them as social constructions by men and for men and to read their "silences" as indications of the historical reality of women about which they do not speak directly. Rather than reject the "argument from silence" as a valid historical argument we have to read carefully the "clues" of the text pointing to a different historical reality and to integrate them into a feminist model of historical reconstruction in such a way that we can "fill" out the silences and understand them as part of the submerged traditions of the egalitarian early Christian movement.[39] Just as other sources, so androcentric biblical texts are part of an overall puzzle and design that have to be "fitted" together in creative critical historical interpretation.

[38] Such a procedure is not restricted to early Christian writers but is found in all forms of historiography. See P. Hernadi, "Clio's Cousins," 247: "The historian tends to see his [sic] evidence as mainly consisting of original texts. Yet all documents at his [sic] disposal, as well as the very work he [sic] is engaged in writing, are translations of the largely *non-verbal* fabric of historical events. . . . Many events, of course, have never been turned into documents and will forever escape the attention of posterity. As a result, the historian may attempt to say 'nothing but the truth' but cannot expect to report 'all the truth.' This is a grave predicament, because as translators and other interpreters of texts know, the meaning of a whole text cannot be reliably construed without reference to the meaning of each part and vice versa."

[39] It is obvious that I am not arguing here for the writing of historical fiction. As we have seen, historical imagination is always at work in interpreting a historical text and reconstructing a historical event. Yet in historiography historical imagination is limited and controlled by the available "evidence," while in fiction it is not. For example, it is

It is crucial, therefore, that we challenge the androcentric model of early Christian history, assuming instead a feminist pattern for the historical mosaic, one that allows us to place women as well as men into the center of early Christian history. Such a feminist critical method could be likened to historical-theological "detective" work in that it does not rely on the obvious "facts" nor "invent" its evidence but is engaged in an imaginative reconstruction of historical reality. Or to use the metaphors of the feminist poet Adrienne Rich: In order to "wrench meaning" from androcentric texts and history we have to "mine" "the earth-deposits of our history" to find the "bottle amber perfect," "the tonic for living on this earth the winters of this climate."[40] Such a feminist hermeneutical method and process for unearthing biblical feminist history, for "entering an old text from a new critical direction" is not just a "chapter in cultural history" but an "act of survival." In deconstructing dominant male language and traditions

> feminist interpretation restores the complexity of historical and symbolic processes. Feminist interpretation draws its strength from recognizing the common tradition as common, the product of many labors and subjectivities. But this recognition in turn compels feminist interpretation to take the tradition seriously and to struggle to appropriate it. The point of feminist interpretation is not to reject the tradition in *toto*, but rather to reappropriate it in the name of those whose participation has been governed by injustice, those who have been excluded not so much from its workings as from its dominant subjective voice.[41]

In conclusion, in order to break the hold of androcentric biblical texts over us, it is necessary to uncover the mechanisms and incoherences of such texts, to see the inconsistencies of our sources, to elaborate the androcentric projections and political-theological functions of such texts and their contemporary androcentric interpretation. In order to recover the historical defeats and victories, sufferings and contributions of our biblical foremothers and foresisters as our own heritage and historical power, we must insist on new feminist models for historical reconstruction.

Such models of historical remembrance must replace the androcentric models of biblical history and help us to re-vision Christian origins and

---

possible to read androcentric New Testament texts as inclusive of women because, on the one hand, we have some clear statements that women as well as men were members of the early Christian communities and, on the other hand, we have no evidence that early Christianity was an exclusively male cult. Why then do translators insist that, for example, the address "brothers" in the Pauline letters must be translated in an androcentric-exclusive way?

[40] See A. Rich, "Natural Resources," in *The Dream of a Common Language: Poems 1974-1977* (New York: Norton, 1978) 60–67.

[41] Elizabeth Fox-Genovese, "For Feminist Interpretation," *Union Seminary Quarterly Review* 35 (1979/80) 13.

biblical theology in a feminist perspective. Biblical history and theology can no longer be done just for men but must be written explicitly also for women. It does not seek an increase in antiquarian information but an increase in historical consciousness and biblical remembrance.

Rather than integrate itself into the Rankean paradigm of historical biblical scholarship, a feminist historical reconstruction of early Christian origins seeks to recover the literary or rhetorical historical paradigm as well as the understanding of history as remembrance and memory for those who are participants in it. The significance of the latter distinction comes clearly to the fore in discussions of the historical event of the Holocaust. Responding to revisionist historians who argue that this event has never taken place,[42] the Jewish historian Pierre Vidal-Naquet has addressed the relationship between history and memory most forcefully. He argues that "today we are witnessing the transformation of memory into history. . . . My generation, people about fifty, is probably the last one for whom Hitler's crimes are still a memory. That both disappearance and, worse still, depreciation of this memory must be combated seems to me obvious. . . . But what are we going to do with this memory, that while it is our memory, is not that of everybody?" But rather than follow the political implications of this statement, he insists on a clear-cut distinction between memory and history. He shares with us that during the war his father had him read Chateaubriand's famous article in the *Mercure* of 4 July 1807, from which he quotes: "In the silence of abjection, when the only sounds to be heard are the chains of the slave and the voice of the informer; when everything trembles before the tyrant . . . this is when the historian appears charged with avenging the people." But Vidal-Naquet disagrees with Chateaubriand about the task of the historian. He insists: "I still believe in the need to remember and, in my way I try to be a man of memory; but I no longer believe that historians are charged with 'avenging the people.' We must accept the fact that the war is over, that the tragedy has become, in a way, secularized. . . ."[43]

Although I would not insist on revenge as the historian's task, I would maintain that history and remembrance should not be separated in such a way "as if the war is over." Anti-Semitism and misogynism are not movements and events of the past. To recover biblical history as

---

[42] Cf. Lucy S. Dawidowicz, "Lies about the Holocaust," *Commentary* 70 (1980) 31–37; cf. also her *The Holocaust and the Historians* (Cambridge, MA: Harvard University Press, 1981).

[43] Pierre Vidal-Naquet, "A Paper Eichmann?" *Democracy* (April 1981) 93–94. For a different interpretation of Vidal-Naquet's position see Hayden White, "The Politics of Historical Interpretation," 136–43. It seems to me that not "meaningfulness" or "meaninglessness" is the issue but historical continuity.

memory and remembrance as history for women would not mean abandoning critical historiography but deepening a critical understanding of historical inquiry that conceives of historiography as a memory and tradition *for* people of today and tomorrow. We stand in the same struggle as our biblical foresisters against the oppression of patriarchy and for survival and freedom from it. We share in the same liberating visions and commitments as our biblical foremothers. We are not called to "empathize" or to "identify" with *their* struggles and hopes but to continue *our* struggle in solidarity with them.[44] Their memory and remembrance—rediscovered and kept alive in historical reconstruction and actualized in ritual celebration—encourage us in historical solidarity with them to commit ourselves to the continuing struggle against patriarchy in society and church.

[44] For "solidarity" as a goal of critical biblical interpretation, see K. Berger, *Exegese des Neuen Testaments* (Uni-Taschenbücher 658; Heidelberg: Quelle & Meyer, 1977) 242–69.

4

EARLY CHRISTIAN WOMEN
AND THEIR CULTURAL CONTEXT: ISSUES OF METHOD IN HISTORICAL RECONSTRUCTION*

Bernadette J. Brooten

If one desires to learn about the lives, practices, and beliefs of early Christian women, one should focus primarily on those women. The vast majority of research on women in early Christianity does not, however, focus primarily on women but rather on what men thought about women. If we want to reconstruct the history of early Christian women, a shift of emphasis is therefore required. We will need to place women in the center of the frame. Placing women in the center means that the categories developed to understand the history of man may no longer be adequate, that the traditional historical periods and canons of literature may not be the proper framework, and that we will need to ask new types of questions and consider hitherto overlooked sources. How and why we study cultural context would shift. If the focus were on women, then one might be less inclined to compare Paul with his male Jewish contemporaries and their views on women and more interested in placing such Roman Jewish women as Prisca and Junia within their Jewish and Roman context.

The approach I am describing is not the only legitimate one. One might study the Pauline passages relating to women in order to understand Paul better or one could examine gospel narratives relating to women so as to come to a better knowledge of the ministry of Jesus. Alternatively, one might attempt a feminist interpretation of a New Testament passage not directly related to women, for feminist interpretation is meant to be comprehensive. The point is not that my approach

* This article was written within the context of the "Frau und Christentum" project of the Institut für ökumenische Forschung, University of Tübingen, West Germany. I would like to thank the Stiftung Volkswagenwerk, which is funding this project, as well as the project-team for providing critical comments, typing the manuscript and doing bibliographical work: Inge Baumann, Christina Bucher, Jutta Flatters, Hans Küng, and Linda Maloney.

is the only legitimate one but rather that the method and the framework should fit the purpose. Since at the present the interest of most New Testament scholars—even of those writing on women in the New Testament—is not in the history of women, then those who have that interest need to reconsider the approach to the study of women current within New Testament scholarship.

This shift in focus also means a change in what one counts as social context and what one sees to be the theological center or revelation. New Testament scholars often locate questions relating to women as part of early Christianity's cultural milieu, part of the social world of the New Testament, but not as central to revelation. When we put women in the center of the frame, then a different constellation of theology, cultural milieu, and social world will emerge. When woman is no longer simply the social and cultural background of the theological center, then a shift in historical method and a rethinking of theology are required.[1]

I. *Early Christian Women's History as Prehistory*

The study of early Christian women is not parallel to the study of early Christian men. To say that women have entered into history and are not simply a part of nature—forming the backdrop, waiting patiently for their husbands to return from the war or the marketplace or the synagogue or the senate, giving birth to sons who make history, mourning the dead and then dying and falling into oblivion themselves, close to life and to death, at one with the eternal cycle of nature—is to contradict the presuppositions of male-centered historiography. The history of man does not allow woman to be a subject of history. It would trivialize the near silence concerning women in our historical sources to create the impression that women's history is parallel to men's history. To consider women's history worthy of study is to go against the grain of traditional history writing. The lack of sources on women is part of the history of women. That we have been hindered from writing or forced to write anonymously or under a man's name, that male historians have considered women's lives unworthy of description, and that that which women have written has usually been ignored by scholars or is no longer extant makes the writing of women's history qualitatively different from the writing of men's history.

To express this qualitative difference, I would like to employ the

---

[1] For an extensive discussion of feminist hermeneutics and an application to early Christianity, see Elisabeth Schüssler Fiorenza, *In Memory of Her: A Feminist Theological Reconstruction of Christian Origins* (New York: Crossroad, 1983), which is the most creative and solid work of its type to date. In the present essay I have purposefully tried to build on Schüssler Fiorenza's work by avoiding extensive treatment of issues that she discusses, focusing instead on other questions.

term "prehistory," a term used by Mary Daly for the history of women.[2] "Prehistory" expresses the radical lack of our knowledge about women in antiquity. The story is nearly entirely missing; we are left with but a few scattered fragments. Yet "prehistory" does not imply that the task is hopeless, that we had best give up, thus letting those who have erased women from history have the last say. It implies a different kind of task, with different methods. To study prehistorical periods is difficult; we will never know as much about life in such periods as in those for which there exist written records. And yet, thorough and careful study of *all* available sources will enable us to reconstruct a much more complete picture than has hitherto been possible. Recognizing that, for women, the state of the sources is similar to that for men and women for the periods usually deemed prehistorical should elicit in us the shock necessary for rethinking the way we use the sources. Sources by men are also primarily about men; they may have little or nothing to do with women's activities or perceptions of themselves. Therefore it is absolutely necessary that we cast the net as widely as possible drawing upon hitherto overlooked sources, such as nonliterary documents (inscriptions, papyri), monumental remains, art, funerary remains, the few literary fragments and works composed by women, as well as women's oral traditions quoted in literary sources.

The term "prehistory" should also serve as a warning to us, for it expresses the highly tentative nature of any reconstruction. If women's history is something different from that which has passed for human history, then the mode of writing must also be different. Traditional historians have tried to create the impression that their reconstructions are firmly rooted in the base of certain and objective knowledge, and scholars of women's history need to beware of similarly objectifying language.[3] The work of women's history must be based upon historical imagination. The thoughts behind a reconstruction would be: Let us imagine that this is the way it was; maybe it was not the way we have always thought, but rather this way. Such a childlike *Leitsatz* may seem to undercut the very foundations of scholarly historical criticism. One might think that careful textual analysis and scientific study of nonliterary remains were about to be replaced by

---

[2] Mary Daly, *Gyn/Ecology: The Metaethics of Radical Feminism* (Boston: Beacon, 1978) 24.

[3] Elizabeth Castelli, unpublished response to Bernadette Brooten, "Inscriptional Evidence for Women as Leaders in the Ancient Synagogue" (Paper delivered at the Claremont New Testament Seminar, Claremont, CA, 28 September 1982).

Among the male scholars who recognize the tentative nature of historiography, see esp. Van A. Harvey, *The Historian and the Believer: The Morality of Historical Knowledge and Christian Belief* (Philadelphia: Westminster, 1966) and Frank Kermode, *The Genesis of Secrecy: On the Interpretation of Narrative* (Cambridge, MA: Harvard University Press, 1979) 101–23.

free-flowing fantasy. This is not the case. Scholars would need to examine each reconstruction, testing the interpretation of each fragment, analyzing the sketched-in lines connecting each fragment, and evaluating the suitability of the chosen framework. The difference would not be between fantastic fiction and secure and certain knowledge but rather between a self-consciously artistic rendering of what the past may have been and a self-proclaimed mirror of or window into the past. The difficulty is that the mirror and the window were never really that. The relatively greater evidence for men's history put together still does not constitute a mirror image of male reality and certainly not of women's reality. Nor is it possible through critical analysis to sift through the sources and, cleansing them of all perspectival distortions, to arrive at an objective view of the past. Some ancient sources would lead us to believe that women either did not exist or that they were beings very marginal to life. No amount of historical-critical work, no amount of taking the *Tendenz* into account will make woman emerge as a subject of history. If women, that is, half the human race, are absent, then such sources can never yield an objective picture of human history. Woman represents a crack in the system; her existence as central and not marginal demonstrates that both the ancient literary sources and contemporary historiography are not the mirrors or windows they claim to be. But women's history is likewise not a mirror, nor will it, added to men's history, become one. It is not a simple complement that makes the picture complete. Women's existence in history, contrasted with the trivialization and marginalization of women in both ancient sources and modern history writing, demonstrates that men's history is also an artistic rendering, sketched from a particular perspective, closely related to the interests, concerns, and background of the historian, but one that should be based upon and responsible to the ancient evidence relating to men. To accept this as a description of what historians do would imply a new kind of humility on our part. We would be more apt to admit its tentative nature and more straightforward in speaking of how our personal backgrounds and interests influence the choice of topic and the types of questions asked of the material.

Much of what I have outlined here as the mode of doing women's history is not new. In biblical hermeneutics, for example, one has long been aware of the role of presuppositions in interpretation, as Rudolf Bultmann's 1957 article, "Ist voraussetzungslose Exegese möglich?"[4] attests. At the interdisciplinary level, especially the work of Thomas Kuhn has brought to the fore the way in which academic institutional structures

---

[4] *Theologische Zeitschrift* 13 (1957) 409–17, and in *Glauben und Verstehen: Gesammelte Aufsätze* (4 vols.; Tübingen: Mohr [Siebeck], 1964–65) 3. 142–50.

affect research presuppositions and results, a view very congenial to the feminist analysis of the way in which male-dominated institutional structures, academic and otherwise, affect the results of academic research.[5] In spite of a theoretical recognition of some of these problems, the practice of writing men's history seldom reflects these insights. The writing of women's history forces issues to the front which might otherwise lie dormant.

II. *A Shift in Categories Is Required*

New Testament scholars have long recognized the necessity of placing the study of women in the New Testament in a historical, cultural context. Book-length studies on women in the New Testament typically begin with a section on women in Judaism and in the Greco-Roman world, and books and articles on such topics as Jesus and women, the household codes, or the Pauline injunction on veiling of women regularly refer to other sources of the period.[6] In fact, on the surface it appears

[5] See esp. Thomas S. Kuhn, *The Structure of Scientific Revolutions* (2d ed.; Chicago: University of Chicago Press, 1970).

[6] For a survey of recent literature, see the review article by Ross S. Kraemer, "Women in the Religions of the Greco-Roman World," *Religious Studies Review* 9 (1983) 127–39. See also the bibliography *Women and Religion: A Select Bibliography* (American Theological Library Association, 1983); and Clare B. Fischer, *Breaking Through: A Bibliography of Women and Religion* (Berkeley, CA: Graduate Theological Union Library, 1980). Of the many works that situate women within their cultural context, two can serve as examples here: Johannes Leipoldt (*Die Frau in der antiken Welt und im Urchristentum* [Berlin and Gütersloh: Mohn, 1962]), who begins with sections on matriarchy, Egyptian women, Roman women, Greek women, and Jewish women (pp. 9–79); and Evelyn and Frank Stagg (*Woman in the World of Jesus* [Philadelphia: Westminster, 1978]), whose "Part I: The World Into Which Jesus Came" includes chapters on the Jewish, Greek, and Roman worlds (pp. 13–100).

Much of the literature on women and the New Testament deals with the question of whether Paul was antifeminist or liberationist, for example, Robin Scroggs, "Paul and the Eschatological Woman," *Journal of the American Academy of Religion* 40 (1972) 283–303; idem, "Paul and the Eschatological Woman: Revisited," *Journal of the American Academy of Religion* 42 (1974) 532–37; response by Elaine H. Pagels, "Paul and Women: A Response to Recent Discussion," *Journal of the American Academy of Religion* 42 (1974) 538–49; G. B. Caird, "Paul and Women's Liberty," *Bulletin of the John Rylands Library* 54 (1972) 268–81; Patrick J. Ford, "Paul the Apostle: Male Chauvinist?" *Biblical Theology Bulletin* 5 (1975) 302–11; A Feuillet, "La dignité et le rôle de la femme d'après quelques textes pauliniens: comparaison avec l'Ancien Testament," *New Testament Studies* 21 (1975) 157–91; A.-M. Dubarle, "Paul et l'antiféminisme," *Revue des sciences philosophiques et théologiques* 60 (1976) 261–80; Veselin Kesich, "St. Paul: Anti-Feminist or Liberator?" *St. Vladimir's Seminary Quarterly* 21 (1977) 123–47; Richard and Joyce Boldrey, *Chauvinist or Feminist? Paul's View of Women* (Grand Rapids, MI: Baker, 1976); Darrell J. Doughty, "Women and Liberation in the Churches of Paul and the Pauline Tradition," *Drew Gateway* 50 (1979) 1–21. For a survey of literature on women and Paul, see Ronald W. Graham, "Women in the Pauline Churches: A Review Article," *Lexington Theological Quarterly* 11 (1976) 25–34.

that on the question of women, more than on many others, scholars recognize that one cannot understand the New Testament in a vacuum.

Upon closer examination, however, several problems emerge that are related to the categories employed. A standard comparison is between women in the New Testament and women in Judaism and the Greco-Roman world (or: women in Rome, Egypt, etc.). In essence, one is comparing statements about women found in a body of literature with statements about women found in the writings of a religious/ethnic group and with those found in the writings of a particular cultural period. In the first century, both Jewish and Christian women were part of the Greco-Roman world. Many Christian women were also Jewish. Another problematic comparison is that between Jewish and Hellenistic, terms which, after the work of V. Tcherikover, E. Bickermann and M. Hengel, can no longer be contrasted with each other.[7] The standard categories of comparison are therefore misleading. This is not simply a formal objection, for the categories chosen determine the very results of research. The sharp contrast usually drawn between women in Judaism and women in early Christianity, for example, is only possible if one fails to recognize that such women as Prisca[8] and Junia,[9] leaders in the early church, were not only Christian but also Jewish and that their activities in leadership probably occurred in the context of a synagogue and thus are part of Jewish women's history.

One of the primary "backgrounds" to the New Testament is the Hellenistic or Greco-Roman world. Problems here emerge both from the way in which it is placed parallel to the Jewish world and from the way in which classicists define the study of women in antiquity from their own discipline. The study of Greek and Roman antiquity has at its root canons of literary excellence. For this reason, departments of classics often limit their course offerings to the core of Greek and Latin literature considered to be the basis of the discipline. Thus, the study of classics is essentially the study of two bodies of literature, and not of a historical period or of a

[7] Victor Tcherikover, *Hellenistic Civilization and the Jews* (Philadelphia: Jewish Publication Society, 1959); Elias Bickerman, *The God of the Maccabees* (Studies in Judaism in Late Antiquity 32; Leiden: Brill, 1979); Martin Hengel, *Judaism and Hellenism* (2d rev. ed.; Philadelphia: Fortress, 1974).

[8] Acts 18:2-3, 24-28; Rom 16:3-5; 1 Cor 16:19; 2 Tim 4:19. On the type of work in which early Christian missionaries such as Prisca were involved and on the cultural context of their work, see esp. Elisabeth Schüssler Fiorenza, *In Memory of Her*, chap. 5: "The Early Christian Missionary Movement: Equality in the Power of the Spirit" (pp. 160-204); idem, "Women in the Pre-Pauline and Pauline Churches," *Union Seminary Quarterly Review* 33 (1978) 156-57.

[9] Rom 16:7. On Junia, see esp. Elisabeth Schüssler Fiorenza, "Die Rolle der Frau in der urchristlichen Bewegung," *Concilium* 12 (1976) 6; Bernadette J. Brooten, "'Junia . . . Outstanding among the Apostles' (Romans 16:7)," in *Women Priests: A Catholic Commentary on the Vatican Declaration* (ed. Leonard Swidler and Arlene Swidler; New York: Paulist, 1977) 141-44.

culture. If history were the primary concern, then other literary traditions of the period, such as Greco-Jewish literature or Aramaic, Demotic or Hebrew literature, would be considered as central as Greek and Latin literature. If the concern were with the development of a culture, then Greek authors of the Roman period or later Latin authors would merit greater attention than they receive. This focus on particular works of Greek and Latin literature within the field of classics has also influenced the study of ancient history, so that Greece and Rome still occupy a preeminent role in courses on ancient history. Further, at least partially because of the existence of the fields of New Testament and patristics, classicists and ancient historians tend to exclude early Christian literature and history from their purview. If this decision were chronologically based, then the related tendency to exclude Jewish literature and history from survey studies would be inexplicable.

For the history of women, this division of labor creates considerable difficulties. The studies on women in classical antiquity tend to cluster around Greece and Rome in their peak periods of literary production, which results in large geographical and chronological gaps.[10] The student of early Christianity, for example, wishing to learn about the history of women in the eastern Roman provinces in the first, second, or third century, will find little. There are a number of studies by classicists on women in Rome in the Republican and Imperial periods, but these do not normally include a discussion of Jewish and Christian women in Rome.[11]

If the study of women in classical antiquity is formed by a field based on literary excellence, the study of women in early Christianity is

---

[10] For literature on women in classical antiquity, see Sarah B. Pomeroy, "Selected Bibliography on Women in Antiquity," *Arethusa* 6 (1973) 125–57; also published in *Women in the Ancient World: The Arethusa Papers* (ed. John Peradotto and J. P. Sullivan; Albany: State University of New York, 1984) 315–42; idem (with Ross S. Kraemer and Natalie Kampen), "Selected Bibliography on Women in Classical Antiquity" in *Women in the Ancient World*, 343–72; Leanna Goodwater, *Women in Antiquity: An Annotated Bibliography* (Metuchen, NJ: Scarecrow, 1975); Sarah B. Pomeroy, *Goddesses, Whores, Wives, and Slaves: Women in Classical Antiquity* (New York: Schocken Books, 1975) 251–59; Marylin B. Arthur, "Classics" (Review Essay), *Signs* 2 (1976) 382–403. For further literature, see the following anthologies: *Arethusa* 6:1 (1973) and 11:1-2 (1978; reprinted as *Women in the Ancient World*); – H. P. Foley, ed., *Reflections of Women in Antiquity* (New York: Gordon and Breach, 1982). For primary sources, see esp. Mary R. Lefkowitz and Maureen B. Fant, *Women's Life in Greece and Rome: A source book in translation* (Baltimore: Johns Hopkins University Press, 1982); Konrad Gaiser, *Für und wider die Ehe: Antike Stimmen zu einer offenen Frage* (Dialog mit der Antike 1; Munich: Heimeran, 1974).

[11] This is reflected in Goodwater (*Women*) both in her selection and within the books and articles reported upon. Some classicists do include a section on Christianity, for example, Lefkowitz and Fant, *Women's Life*, 262–78; Pomeroy, "Bibliography on Women in Antiquity," 149–52; "Bibliography on Women in Classical Antiquity," 365–69 (section prepared by Ross S. Kraemer); but I know of no such inclusion of Judaism.

built upon a discipline shaped by a religious decision. It is the decision of a male-dominated church leadership to canonize the twenty-seven books of the New Testament, which has determined the boundaries of the study of women in early Christianity for most scholars. Further, because both fields are based on bodies of literature, the focus of study tends to be on the images of women in male-authored literary works rather than on the history of women. In addition, a disjuncture exists because, although the Greco-Roman world contains Judaism and Christianity within it, classicists, ancient historians, as well as scholars in Jewish studies and New Testament seldom behave as if this were the case. Because Judaism and Christianity were the only Greco-Roman religions to survive, they merit separate categories of study in contemporary scholarship, and because the classical literature of Greece and of Rome has been so influential on Western thought, they too are given special institutional support today. One must ask whether these divisions are appropriate to the women's history of that period. Much more interdisciplinary cooperation is required to fill in the gaps in research; such cooperation will involve overcoming considerable disciplinary prejudices.

Within the study of women and the cultural context of early Christianity, the assessment of the relative status of women in Judaism and Christianity is particularly problematic and therefore deserves special attention. In a word, on the question of women Judaism is regularly used as a negative backdrop against which to view early Christianity. I am using the terms "status of women" and "question of women" quite consciously, because they accurately describe the approach of most scholars who compare women in ancient Judaism with women in early Christianity; that is, the interest is not in the history of Jewish women, but rather in a comparison between Jewish men and Christian men and their attitudes toward women. Such comparisons usually occur when assessing Jesus' or Paul's attitudes toward women. George Tavard, for example, in discussing 1 Cor 11:2–7 (on the man as the head of the woman, on veiling, and on man being the image and glory of God), writes: "This is patently a very rabbinic passage. Paul has not yet emancipated himself (and how could he have done so?) from the thought patterns of his Jewish-pharisaic training." His comment on the command that women be silent in the churches is: "This old-fashioned Jewish position is hardly in keeping with the principle and the practice of prophecy."[12] G. W. Trompf, referring to Paul's collegial relationship with women, writes: "If Paul had so eluded the patriarchal attitudes of his Jewish inheritance, then, it makes it the more unlikely that 1 Cor 11:3-16 is from his

---

[12] George H. Tavard, *Woman in Christian Tradition* (Notre Dame, IN: University of Notre Dame Press, 1973) 29, 30.

hand."[13] Tavard does not say how the passage from 1 Corinthians 11 is rabbinic (in midrashic technique? are there rabbinic parallels?), nor does he document that the prohibition of women speaking in religious services is in fact a Jewish position. Further, the juxtaposition of Jewish and prophetic is a rather curious one. Trompf similarly makes a simple equation between patriarchal and Jewish, implying that for Paul to work together with women was to go beyond his Jewish inheritance.

The difficulties in the comparative study of women in Judaism and Christianity are inherent not only in such offhanded comments, left undocumented and unexplained, but also in the conceptual framework within which one studies women in ancient Judaism. One major problem is the confusion of prescriptive with descriptive literature; that is, one takes rabbinic sayings about women to be a reflection of Jewish women's reality. Concomitant with this lack of distinction is the organization of the study according to literary corpus. Evelyn and Frank Stagg, in their book *Woman in the World of Jesus*,[14] for example, arrange the section on women in the Jewish world according to "Philo of Alexandria," "The Writings of Josephus," etc. They follow the same literary rubric in their sections on women in the Greek and Roman worlds. Such an arrangement lends itself to woman being treated as a literary motif and to a confusion between images of women in Jewish literature and the history of Jewish women. The focus is on male writers and their attitudes toward women, rather than on women themselves. Given this literary outline, with its accompanying lack of attention to nonliterary sources, it is not surprising that literature is confused with reality.

One example of this is a statement in the section on the Mishnah: "In Jewish society, divorce was a man's prerogative, not a woman's (*Yeb.* 14.1), except in the relatively rare cases where a woman wielded special power, as in the more Roman than Jewish Herodian families."[15] In discussing Jesus' prohibition of divorce, they note: "One thing common to all passages ascribed to Jesus is the absence of the double standard that discriminated against woman."[16] If one studies the problem of Jewish divorce historically, drawing upon all available evidence rather than only the few readily known texts, it becomes evident that there were two strands of legal thought and practice in ancient Judaism. According to the one, only the man could initiate a divorce, but according to the other a woman also had that right.[17] If that is the background, then the question of the double

[13] G. W. Trompf, "On Attitudes Toward Women in Paul and Paulinist Literature: 1 Corinthians 11:3-16 and Its Context," *Catholic Biblical Quarterly* 42 (1980) 211.

[14] See above, n. 6. In spite of the questions I raise here, this book is helpful in many ways.

[15] Stagg, *Woman in the World of Jesus*, 51.

[16] Stagg, *Woman in the World of Jesus*, 133.

[17] For documentation and discussion of the evidence for ancient Jewish divorce practice

standard may not have been Jesus' concern at all. Further, the strict prohibition of divorce has worked not only to protect women from arbitrary dismissal by their husbands but also to lock women into unhappy and even violent marriages. A total prohibition of divorce in the context of patriarchal marriage cannot be seen as simply liberating for women.

Evelyn and Frank Stagg are by no means alone in viewing Jesus' prohibition of divorce in this way. Leonard Swidler speaks of "Jesus' revolutionary egalitarian attitude toward women in marriage by eliminating the husband's right to divorce his wife,"[18] and Johannes Leipoldt sees the prohibition as based on love of neighbor and given for the purpose of protecting the woman from ending up in misery.[19] Taken within its own context and within the context of later centuries, Jesus' prohibition of divorce is ambivalent for women. On the one hand, it has protected women from simply being sent away by their husbands. On the other, strictly forbidding divorce changes the nature of marriage, and patriarchal marriage without exit means something rather different for women than for men. Could it be a recognition, perhaps unconscious, of this ambivalence that has led to wanting to see Jesus' prohibition of divorce against the backdrop of inegalitarian Jewish practice of divorce? Could it be that only against that backdrop it seems egalitarian? In her article "Blaming the Jews for the Birth of Patriarchy," Judith Plaskow speaks of projection onto "the Other" of that which we cannot acknowledge in ourselves. She writes: "Feminist research projects onto Judaism the failure of the Christian tradition unambiguously to renounce sexism. . . . This is the real motive behind biased presentations of Jesus' Jewish background: to allow the feminist to present the 'true' Christian tradition as uniquely free from sexism."[20] The treatment of Jewish divorce in the time of Jesus seems to me to be an example of such a projection. Jewish women and their history evoke little attention in all of this; it is at most Jewish men who are of interest as a backdrop for Jesus' saying.

Leonard Swidler has had a long-term commitment to feminist issues within the church and has made important contributions, through his teaching, writing, and editorial activity, in this area. His studies of

---

with respect to women, see the recent debate in *Evangelische Theologie*: Bernadette Brooten, "Konnten Frauen im alten Judentum die Scheidung betreiben? Überlegungen zu Mk 10,11-12 und 1 Kor 7,10-11," *EvT* 42 (1982) 65–80; Eduard Schweizer, "Scheidungsrecht der jüdischen Frau? Weibliche Jünger Jesu?" *EvT* 42 (1982) 294–97 (= "I. B. Brooten"); Hans Weder, "Perspektive der Frauen?" *EvT* 43 (1983) 175–78; Bernadette J. Brooten, "Zur Debatte über das Scheidungsrecht der jüdischen Frau," *EvT* 43 (1983) 466–78.

[18] Leonard Swidler, *Biblical Affirmations of Woman* (Philadelphia: Westminster, 1979) 238.

[19] Leipoldt, *Die Frau in der antiken Welt*, 89.

[20] In *Nice Jewish Girls: A Lesbian Anthology* (ed. Evelyn Torton Beck; Watertown, MA: Persephone Press, 1982) 253; the article appeared previously in *Cross Currents* 28 (1978) 306–9, and in *Lilith* 7. 11–13.

women in ancient Judaism and early Christianity have been more influential on a broad scale over the past decade than the work of any other single scholar, and they are therefore deserving of special attention.[21] There are certain points at which one must raise questions. Swidler's thesis that Jesus was a feminist, which is central to his writing on women in the Bible and women in postbiblical Judaism, rests on his conception of what it meant to be a Jewish woman at the time of Jesus. His focus is on attitudes toward women rather than on the history of Jewish women; this is in keeping with the ultimate goal, which is a comparison between Jesus and other male Jews of his time. This focus is evident in the categories Swidler employs. In *Biblical Affirmations of Woman*, the sections "Woman in Hebrew-Jewish Tradition" and "Woman in Christian Tradition" are subdivided into "positive," "ambivalent," and "negative" (elements, images and/or attitudes). This is not a historical categorization. Were one to be interested primarily in concrete Jewish women, their daily lives, rituals, achievements, and struggles, one would not utilize such categories. For how could one evaluate the complex historical phenomena of Jewish women's lives with the categories "positive," "ambivalent," and "negative"? Even as categories for describing attitudes, these are not adequate. While it is relatively clear what constitutes a negative element or attitude toward women, that which is positive is much less clear. For example, Swidler places Jesus' prohibition of divorce in the "positive" category,[22] but most feminists would disagree that a strict prohibition of divorce is positive for women. Further, his placing the creation of Eve from the rib of Adam and the Fall story (Genesis 2–3) in the "positive" category[23] would hardly meet with unanimous agreement among feminists. The problematic character of Swidler's categories becomes especially evident through his use of the term "ambivalent"; the necessity of this third category makes it clear that these divisions really do not work. "Ambivalent" is a catchall term, situated between "positive" and "negative," subsuming whatever does not fit elsewhere, whereby the lines are often blurred. The section "Deutero-Pauline (and Other) Ambivalent (and Some Negative) Attitudes Toward Women"[24] is a good illustration of the problem. Within that section it is not at all clear which are the ambivalent and which are the negative attitudes. One is also surprised to find that, for example, 1 Cor 14:33b–35, the command that women be silent in the churches, is placed in this category, rather than in the clearly negative one. Swidler, by way of explanation of the pas-

---

[21] Leonard Swidler, "Jesus was a Feminist," *The Catholic World* 212 (Jan. 1971) 171–83; idem, *Women in Judaism: The Status of Women in Formative Judaism* (Metuchen, NJ: Scarecrow, 1976); idem, *Biblical Affirmations*.
[22] *Biblical Affirmations*, 173–75, 238–39, 259.
[23] *Biblical Affirmations*, 76–84.
[24] *Biblical Affirmations*, 332–38.

sage, notes: "Perhaps the author thought of the women as all converts from Judaism, where women for the most part were kept illiterate."[25] The relationship between literacy and public speaking is not a simple one, and the present state of research does not allow us in any case to come to a conclusion about the comparative literacy rate among Diaspora Jewish and Gentile women.

Especially striking about Swidler's outline is that, whereas passages from the Hebrew Bible and extracanonical Jewish writings do fall under the category "negative," on the Christian side, all of the New Testament falls into "positive" or "ambivalent, " and it is only the Christian fathers who are placed in the negative category. The New Testament canon, with the exception of the "(and Some Negative)," is thus kept within the boundaries of the positive and the ambivalent. None of the genuine Pauline passages is considered negative, not even Rom 1:26 (condemnatory evaluation of sexual love relations between women),[26] nor 1 Cor 11:2–16 (veiling of women, subordinationist theology of the sexes).[27]

Especially evident in Swidler, but also at the base of many scholars' work on women in ancient Judaism, is the assumption that quantity within the sources somehow reflects historical reality. This balance-sheet type of approach creates the impression that the sixty-three tractates of the Talmud reflect a greater historical reality than the Jewish inscriptions from Rome (a Jewish community that flourished throughout the Roman period but the literature of which is not extant) or the literary fragments from Alexandria. Although it is true for men's history as well, for women's history one must be exceptionally careful to recall that each mention of women we have is but the tip of an iceberg. If that is the case, then one cannot simply line up all of the Jewish and Christian evidence about women, placing all varieties of sources together and not distinguishing their relative significance.

It is also problematic that Swidler employs the categories "Jewish" and "Hellenistic" throughout his work, as do most Christian scholars who write about Jewish women. The assumption is usually that the Hellenistic world was more progressive and the Jewish world more conservative with respect to women, so that when one discovers progressive elements in Judaism, the tendency is to attribute these to Hellenistic influence. A

---

[25] *Biblical Affirmations*, 337.

[26] Rom 1:26 is mentioned only in passing (p. 330) and does not merit a paragraph of its own. This is not in keeping with the widespread discussions in the women's movement of lesbian existence and discrimination against lesbians.

[27] *Biblical Affirmations*, 329–32.

good example of this is Johannes Leipoldt's treatment of the Therapeutrides, a group of ascetic Jewish women who devoted their lives to
the study of the Torah and the allegorical interpretation thereof (Philo,
De vita contemplativa). Leipoldt writes:

> That it is expressly emphasized that the Therapeutrides are filled
> with the same zeal for the Law as their male colleagues is, however,
> un-Jewish. . . . The Therapeutai are outsiders within Judaism.
> Their ascetic stance . . . is Greek, as is their love of monasti-
> cism. . . . Therefore one cannot view the participation of the
> Therapeutrides in religious services as characteristic for the Jewish
> manner. It remains the case that in general the Jew did not view
> woman as equal to man before God and therefore did not let her
> speak in religious services.[28]

Swidler writes: "The misogynism of much of contemporary Palestinian Judaism seems to have been greatly modified by Greek influence in
the Therapeutae. . . ."[29] In all of this it is not clear that the Thera-
peutrides/ai were outsiders in Judaism at all—Philo praises them highly
and says that they were spread throughout the Greek and the barbarian
worlds (*De vita contemplativa* 21)—nor is it evident why it should be
uncharacteristic of Judaism for women to participate in religious
services.[30] Further, why should foreign influence have been necessary to
counteract Jewish misogynism? Why could Judaism not have been a
pluriform entity, with many strands of thought and variety in practice?

The type of evaluation given by Leipoldt and Swidler is relevant for
New Testament studies in that it excludes from the discussion evidence
of Jewish women's intellectual activity by a priori ruling it out of court
as being non-Jewish in origin. This in turn results in the view that
women in ancient Judaism were nearly always victims of male dominance and seldom leaders or contributors to culture. A view of women in
Judaism from which the progressive elements have been cleansed as
being Hellenistic in origin is then taken as the backdrop for New Testament statements on women.

For Leipoldt the assumption that pagan is more progressive than
Jewish goes so far that he discusses Lydia and Prisca in the context of
Gentile Christians, noting: "After all of that it is not surprising that
Christian women are mentioned and praised relatively more frequently
in the Gentile church than in Jerusalem."[31] According to Acts 16:13–15,

[28] Leipoldt, *Die Frau in der antiken Welt*, 59, 60, 61 (my translation); discussed by
Swidler, *Women in Judaism*, 66–69; *Biblical Affirmations*, 133–34.

[29] Swidler, *Women in Judaism*, 69; *Biblical Affirmations*, 134.

[30] On women's participation in synagogue worship services, see Bernadette J. Brooten,
*Women Leaders in the Ancient Synagogue: Inscriptional Evidence and Background
Issues* (Brown Judaic Studies 36; Chico, CA: Scholars Press, 1982) 139–41.

[31] Leipoldt, *Die Frau in der antiken Welt*, 109 (my translation).

Paul met Lydia at the sabbath synagogue service,[32] and Acts 18:2 reports that Priscilla and Aquila were Jews. (Compare Acts 18:26, in which Priscilla and Aquila are said to have taught the Jewish rhetor Apollos in a synagogue context.)

One of the most widely read brief studies on women in ancient Judaism is the appendix on the topic by Joachim Jeremias in *Jerusalem in the Time of Jesus*.[33] Although it is much more extensively documented than any of the literature cited thus far and less inaccurate in detail, there are nevertheless certain structural difficulties. Similar to the other authors, Jeremias's primary interest is not in Jewish women but in contrasting Jesus with his male Jewish contemporaries, as his closing paragraphs indicate. One of the major points of contrast is Jesus' prohibition of divorce.[34] This focus on Jesus determines the way in which he describes the position of Jewish women. He places special emphasis on statements concerning subordination and restriction, of which there are many, and tends to take them as simple reflections of historical reality. Jewish evidence attesting to anything other than the subordination of women he rarely quotes or examines critically. One example of this would be the inscriptional occurrence of the title *archisynagōgos*, "head of the synagogue," for women, which Jeremias declares to have occurred under foreign influence and to be honorific, a view for which there is little evidence in the sources.[35]

In order to come to a better historical understanding of the material with which Jeremias deals, most of which is rabbinic, one would need first of all to study it systemically in its literary context. Jacob Neusner has provided a model for such work in his five-volume commentary on Mishnah's Division on Women.[36] Such systemic study is not an attempt to excuse or apologize for the misogyny found in rabbinic texts, as Neusner's work amply demonstrates. On the contrary, it helps to locate and understand rabbinic statements concerning women within the male-centered thought system from which they emanate. As a historian of

---

[32] The RSV and some other translations do not translate *proseuchē* in Acts 16:13 as "synagogue." This hesitancy is in part due to the fact that it was women who were gathered there. *Proseuchē*, however, is well attested as meaning "synagogue." On this problem of terminology see Martin Hengel, "Proseuche und Synagoge. Jüdische Gemeinde, Gotteshaus und Gottesdienst in der Diaspora und in Palästina," in *Festschrift Karl Georg Kuhn: Tradition und Glaube* (ed. Gert Jeremias, Heinz-Wolfgang Kuhn and Hartmut Stegemann; Göttingen: Vandenhoeck & Ruprecht, 1971) 157–84; Paul Wexler, "Terms for 'Synagogue' in Hebrew and Jewish Languages: Explorations in Historical Jewish Interlinguistics," *Revue des études juives* 140 (1981) 101–38; Brooten, *Women Leaders*, 139–40.

[33] Joachim Jeremias, *Jerusalem in the Time of Jesus* (Philadelphia: Fortress, 1969) 358–76.

[34] Jeremias, *Jerusalem*, 376.

[35] Jeremias, *Jerusalem*, 374 n. 79; see Brooten, *Women Leaders*, 5–39, 223–33.

[36] Jacob Neusner, *A History of the Mishnaic Law of Women* (5 vols.; Leiden: Brill, 1980).

women, one needs to remember that such a system does not correspond to historical reality. As Neusner puts it: "So Mishnah speaks for its authorities and tells us what is on their minds, that alone. Only in later times would the Israelite world come to approximate, and even conform to, Mishnah's vision of reality. But the meaning of which we presently speak is in the minds of a handful of men."[37]

What Neusner means is that the rabbinic authorities, the teachers whose sayings are recorded in the Mishnah, began as a small group of men whose understanding of Judaism came to be accepted as normative only in later centuries. The sayings of the rabbis do not reflect historical reality, but rather their vision of reality, and need to be studied in the context of that vision. The next step after systemically analyzing the rabbinic understanding of women and differentiating with respect to individual rabbis' views would be to begin to reconstruct Jewish women's history in antiquity. The focus would be on Jewish women, rather than as at present on Jewish men's attitudes, and the purpose would be to understand the history of Jewish women better, rather than to use Judaism as a mere backdrop against which to view early Christianity. Such an approach would also be much more useful for those whose primary interest is early Christianity, because fuller, more complete, more critical history of Jewish women in antiquity would provide a much better basis than we have now for placing early Christian women in their historical context and for comparative studies.[38]

III. *Restructuring Implies New Questions and a New Framework*

What concrete shape might the history of early Christian women take?[39] How might one proceed with it? In order to reconstruct this

[37] Jacob Neusner, *Method and Meaning in Ancient Judaism* (Brown Judaic Studies 10; Missoula, MT: Scholars Press, 1979) 95.

[38] For further discussion of the study of women in Judaism on the part of Christian scholars, see Bernadette J. Brooten, "Jüdinnen zur Zeit Jesu. Ein Plädoyer für Differenzierung," *Theologische Quartalschrift* (Tübingen) 161 (1981) 281–85. An important project in progress at present is that being undertaken by Ross S. Kraemer on the topic of women in Greek-speaking Jewish communities in the Roman Empire. Kraemer follows an approach similar to that outlined below, that is, a women's history approach. For further literature on the history of Jewish women in antiquity, see esp. Ora Hamelsdorf and Sandra Adelsberg, *Jewish Women and Jewish Law* (Fresh Meadows, NY: Biblio, 1980). For the older literature, see Bernhard Wachstein, *Literatur über die jüdische Frau* (Veröffentlichungen der Bibliothek der israelitischen Kultusgemeinde Wien 7; Vienna: Bibliothek der israelitischen Kultusgemeinde, 1931).

[39] Those working on women's history in early Christianity can benefit greatly from historians of women of other periods. See, for example, Mary R. Beard, *Woman as Force in History: A Study in Traditions and Realities* (New York: Macmillan, 1962); *Conceptual Frameworks For Studying Women's History*: four papers by: Marylin Arthur, Renate Bridenthal, Joan Kelly-Gadol, Gerda Lerner (A Sarah Lawrence College Women's Studies

history, one would need to have a good understanding of social, political, and economic conditions of the women of various classes in all parts of the Roman Empire; of women's participation in and the theology of other Greco-Roman religions, including Judaism; of first-century philosophical and religious thinking about women; of the laws affecting women in the various geographical regions; of women's participation in public life, including politics; of sexual behavior and attitudes toward sexuality; and of the physical living conditions of women, that is, architecture, art, ceramics, etc. One would want to know how many women could write, what women's education consisted of, what women wore, and what kinds of work slave women did. It would be necessary to note developments within women's history in the first century, tracing them back to and/or contrasting them with previous centuries. A study of first-century Christian women would also imply a study of first-century Christian men's theology and practice, as well as of such societal institutions as the family. All of this requires a new kind of synthesis, drawing upon New Testament and Jewish studies, classics, ancient history, archaeology, art history, papyrology, epigraphy, and anthropology.[40]

A history of Christian women in the first century would be a history of women, and not a history of male attitudes toward women. If the primary focus were on women, then the history of Christian women would be part not only of the history of early Christianity but also of the history of first-century women. One would not just be comparing Paul's statements on women with Philo's statements on women; one would be locating women like Junia and Prisca in the continuum of Jewish women's history, which includes the Therapeutrides, Jewish women who

Publication, 1975); Berenice A. Carroll, ed., *Liberating Women's History: Theoretical and Critical Essays* (Urbana: University of Illinois Press, 1976); Joan Kelly-Gadol, "The Social Relation of the Sexes: Methodological Implications of Women's History," *Signs* 1 (1976) 809–23; Sheila Rowbotham, *Hidden from History: Rediscovering Women in History from the 17th Century to the Present* (New York: Random House, 1976); Carolyn C. Lougee, "Modern European History" (Review Essay), *Signs* 2 (1977) 628–50; Gerda Lerner, *The Majority Finds Its Past: Placing Women in History* (Oxford: Oxford University Press, 1979); articles in the journal *Pénélope* 1- (1979-); Christine Fauré, "Absent from History," *Signs* 7 (1981) 71–80; idem, "The Twilight of the Goddesses, or The Intellectual Crisis of French Feminism," *Signs* 7 (1981) 81–86; Carl N. Degler, "What the Women's Movement Has Done to American History," *Soundings* 44 (1981) 403–21; Jane Lewis, "Women, Lost and Found: The Impact of Feminism on History," in *Men's Studies Modified: The Impact of Feminism on the Academic Disciplines* (ed. Dale Spender; Oxford and New York: Pergamon, 1981) 55–72; Gisela Bock, "Historische Frauenforschung: Fragestellungen und Perspektiven," in *Frauen suchen ihre Geschichte* (ed. Karin Hausen; Munich: Beck, 1983) 22–60.
[40] On the usefulness of anthropological research for the study of women's history, see esp. Gianna Pomata, "Die Geschichte der Frauen zwischen Anthropologie und Biologie," *Feministische Studien* 2:2 (1983) 113–27.

were synagogue leaders, and Beruriah.[41] Junia and Prisca were both
first-century Roman Jewish women. Prisca taught in a context related to
the synagogue (Acts 18:26); had a house church together with her husband Aquila (Rom 16:5; 1 Cor 16:19), with whom she also worked as a
tent maker (Acts 18:3); and, according to Acts 18:2, was banned from
Rome and went to Corinth. Junia was an apostle, a fellow prisoner of
Paul, and had become a Christian before Paul (Rom 16:7). A study of
Junia and Prisca in their historical context would therefore mean posing
such questions as: What are the sources for first-century Jewish women
in Rome? What do we know about women and the Roman penal code?
What do we know about Jewish women's education and about non-
Jewish Roman women's education in this period? Are there other examples of wives and husbands practicing a trade together? What would
have been the income from such a trade? How much do we know about
women and travel in this period? Did women serve as delegates or missionaries in other religious movements or in civic contexts? What can we
know of the size, layout, and cost of a house in which a house church
could have met? These questions are rather straightforward historical
questions, unusual only because they simply presuppose that women, like
men, are historical beings, and that the historical study of women is a
worthwhile enterprise.

To write women's history cannot, however, mean to use literature as
a sort of attic archive, drawing out historical details and pasting together
a collage which then passes as historical reality. The historian must
respect the integrity of literature, recognizing that the very historicity of
a literary document implies studying it for itself, in its present form,
with its own contours. It would, therefore, be inappropriate to search the
New Testament for snippets of information about women, cutting them
out and placing them side by side with similar snippets about other first-
century women painstakingly clipped from other literary and nonliterary sources, glueing the whole thing together and passing it off as
the reality of women's lives in the first century. This is not the enterprise. Junia and Prisca were both associates of Paul, and they cannot be
understood apart from him. In fact, were it not for Paul, we would know
nothing of Junia and even less of Prisca than we do know. To say that
Junia and Prisca were Paul's associates is, however, not to say that they
shared his theology, Christology, or understanding of women. But it is to
say that Paul's desire that women be veiled while preaching or prophesying and the accompanying idea that God is the head of Christ, Christ

[41] Beruriah was a learned Palestinian Jewish woman of the early second century. See
esp. David Goodblatt, "The Beruriah Traditions," *Journal of Jewish Studies* 26 (1975)
68–85.

the head of the man, and the man the head of the woman (1 Cor 11:2–16)[42] were part of their reality. They may not have accepted Paul's views for themselves or they may have. In any case they probably could not ignore them, and Paul's views are therefore a part of their history and must be analyzed as such. Such an analysis would, however, be of a new type. Rather than taking Paul's views on women as an accurate reflection of early Christian women's reality, one would analyze Paul's system of thought on its own terms and in the context of male thinking of the time and then ask how women in antiquity were affected by and, in turn, how they affected Paul's views. On the question of veiling, for example, 1 Cor 11:2–16 is evidence that some women did not agree with Paul. It was presumably their refusing to wear the sign of submission that caused Paul to write on the subject and to formulate a theology of headship as theoretical support for the practice of veiling. Whether the Corinthian women finally accepted either Paul's subordinationist theology or his command that they be veiled, we do not know.

To write women's history, to place women at the center, is to say that men are not at the center of reality, that what men do and are is not more important than what women do and are. It is still true, for both general and church history, that the topics chosen and the questions asked assume that men's activities and thoughts are more important than women's. The tendency to emphasize political and military history is based on this assumption, as is the tendency in church history to focus on the history of councils, papal pronouncements, and dogmas. When the framework is structured in this way, it is not surprising to find the history of women subsumed under such categories as "the role of women," or "the status of women." Such terminology evokes the image of the landscape of a male reality that is varied and complex. Men have many roles, and their reality varies as to social class, geographical region, race, religion, historical period, etc. Into this dynamic and active landscape, we now place woman, a clay figurine, which is put into place at some

[42] On 1 Cor 11:2–16, see esp. Morna D. Hooker, "Authority on Her Head: An Examination of I Cor xi.10," *New Testament Studies* 10 (1964–65) 410–16; Robin Scroggs, "Paul and the Eschatological Woman," *Journal of the American Academy of Religion* 40 (1972) 297–302; Annie Jaubert, "Le voile des femmes (1 Cor xi. 2–16)," *New Testament Studies* 18 (1972) 419–30; William O. Walker, "1 Corinthians 11:2–16 and Paul's Views Regarding Women," *Journal of Biblical Literature* 94 (1975) 94–110; A. Feuillet, "La dignité et le rôle de la femme d'après quelques textes pauliniens," *New Testament Studies* 21 (1975) 157–91; Jerome Murphy-O'Connor, "The Non-Pauline Character of 1 Corinthians 11:2–16?" *Journal of Biblical Literature* 95 (1976) 615–21; John P. Meier, "On the Veiling of Hermeneutics (1 Cor 11:2–16)," *Catholic Biblical Quarterly* 40 (1978) 212–26; Lamar Cope, "1 Cor 11:2–16: One Step Further," *Journal of Biblical Literature* 97 (1978) 435–36; Jerome Murphy-O'Connor, "Sex and Logic in 1 Corinthians 11:2–16," *Catholic Biblical Quarterly* 42 (1980) 482–500; Schüssler Fiorenza, *In Memory of Her*, 226–30, 233.

one point in the moving scene. One can now discuss her role, her status, her relation to men in the scene. If, as the discussion proceeds, one notices that woman actually has several roles or that the status of a slave woman in the society in question differs from the status of an aristocratic woman, one adds new clay figurines to the scene to express that diversity. One can also place this landscape next to others and compare the status of woman in one society with the status of woman in another. This clay-figurine method of the study of women is really based on the view that women are not active participants in history at all, but rather passive recipients of a role or roles given to them by men and a status allowed to them by men. Placing women in the center means that the clay figurines come alive. They begin to talk to each other, telling their experiences, their beliefs, their hopes, their theories, and their opinions.

In the context of male-dominated society (which is not to be equated with male-centered reality), to place women in the center is not the same as the male-centered landscape shadow boxes we have been viewing. To place women at the center is not "reverse discrimination." Focusing in on the clay figurines and wanting to hear them is the only way to allow them to come alive. To listen to women is not to refuse to hear men; it is to let those who have been mute speak.

One might object that this is all a rather idealized picture: the clay figurines of the past come alive and begin telling us their story with great animation and even in dialogue with each other. I must quickly add that such a thing cannot ever happen in quite this way for antiquity. We will probably never hear the women of early Christianity in their discussing, debating, and struggling with or in their comforting one another. The most we can hope for is a snippet of a conversation, a quick glimpse through a crack in the door. If we do not focus all of our attention on how to get that snippet and that glimpse, we will miss them.

In order to be prepared to receive, we must phrase the questions properly. If we ask about military affairs, governmental intrigues or the development of church hierarchy, the din of male voices will drown out the one or two women speaking. If, on the other hand, we ask about popular piety; look at the pictures people venerated; talk about taxes, work, and wages; marriage, divorce, and celibacy; spinning and weaving and clothing and food; if we ask what women read and wrote, what they said, and what they did, then we may hear what the women have to tell us.

With this kind of framework, it should be clear that comparisons between early Christianity and its cultural context would not be comparisons of the status and role of women. The purpose of comparing early Christianity with other religious movements and of setting it in its cultural context would be to understand the language in which early Christian women spoke and to be able to imagine what their lives may have been like. In order to understand why women may have become Christian, one would want to know as much as possible about the women and men who did not become Christians, as well as about the men who did. With such a model, the study of women would no longer be a battleground for the struggle over the superiority of one religion over another; this would not, however, mean an avoidance of questions of meaning.

If framework implies where women are placed in the picture, it also entails the question of historical periodization, that is, the boundaries of each frame. Women's historians have called into question the traditional periodization of history as not necessarily reflecting women's experience. As Joan Kelly-Gadol put it: "Let me merely point out that if we apply Fourier's famous dictum—that the emancipation of women is an index of the general emancipation of an age—our notions of so-called progressive developments, such as classical Athenian civilization, the Renaissance, and the French Revolution, undergo a startling re-evaluation."[43] It was, in fact, Kelly-Gadol's negative answer to the question "Did Women Have a Renaissance?" which introduced periodization as an issue in women's history.[44] We might ask whether, for example, "History of the Jewish people in the Period of the Mishnah and the Talmud" is the best framework within which to place Jewish women's history from ca. the first century B.C.E. through the sixth century C.E. "Apostolic Age," which presumably does not include Junia (Rom 16:7) or Thecla, who is called an apostle in some traditions, also needs to be questioned as a period of Christian women's history, as does the "Patristic Period." For the time being, the political designations ("Ptolemaic," "Roman," "Byzantine," etc.) may prove to be the most useful. Changes in government meant changes in law, which did affect women's lives. In Ptolemaic Egypt, for example, women could not own land, but in Roman Egypt they could. Similarly, the advent of the Christian emperors meant legal changes that significantly affected women's lives, such as in the area of divorce law. Nevertheless, these political periods should be understood merely as convenient markers. One would still need to examine whether there might be more important turning points in ancient women's history than changes in political power. For religious history, it may be best to suspend the use of periods for the time being and to speak simply of the century or centuries involved.

A further area relating to framework is that of canons of literature. The historical study of women cannot limit itself to bodies of literature

---

[43] Kelly-Gadol, "Social Relation," 810–11.

[44] Joan Kelly-Gadol, "Did Women Have a Renaissance?" in *Becoming Visible: Women in European History* (ed. Renate Bridenthal and Claudia Koonz; Boston: Houghton Mifflin, 1977) 137–64. On the question of periodization, see also Lerner, *The Majority Finds Its Past*, 154–59; Degler, "What the Women's Movement Has Done," 418–19.

canonized by men or raised to the level of normativity by men. Within the scope of the present discussion this issue would relate primarily to the history of women in early Christianity and ancient Judaism. Concretely this means that those wishing to study the history of women in early Christianity cannot limit themselves to the New Testament canon and cannot exclude the early Christian churches considered heretical by other branches of early Christianity. For Judaism, the history of Greek- and Latin-speaking Jewish women deserves the same attention as that which one can learn from rabbinic literature, and it should be studied as having its own integrity and not simply interpreted in light of rabbinic halakah and sayings about women. For both Judaism and Christianity, a limitation to the canonical and the normative would yield a skewed picture of women. Were one, for example, to limit oneself to the canonical Pauline and deutero-Pauline literature, one could have the impression that Paul was ambivalent with respect to women, and that this ambivalence was solved by his disciples in the direction of conservatism. One would note that, on the one hand, Paul accepted women as colleagues (Rom 16:1–12; Phil 4:2–3; Phlm 2), believed that gender distinctions cease in Christ (Gal 3:28), accepted women's prophesying activity (1 Cor 11:5), and saw the celibate state as an option for women (1 Cor 7), but that the same Paul required women to wear a veil when praying or prophesying and employed a subordinationist theology and anthropology to justify the practice (1 Cor 11:2–16), prohibited divorce (1 Cor 7:10–11), viewed love relations between women as the result of idolatry (Rom 1:26), and possibly believed that women should be silent in the church assembly (1 Cor 14:34–36—if this is not an interpolation).

Within the canon, the movement of those who see themselves in the tradition of Paul displays increasing subordinationism. The Colossian and Ephesian household codes command women to be subordinate to their husbands, while at the same time commanding husbands to love their wives (Col 3:18–19; Eph 5:22–33), while the Pastoral Epistles argue that woman should learn in silence and should not teach or have authority over a man (1 Tim 2:11–12); woman was second in the order of creation (1 Tim 2:13); Eve was deceived, but Adam was not (1 Tim 2:14); women will be saved by childbearing (1 Tim 2:15); women deacons (or wives of deacons?) should be serious, not slanderers, temperate and faithful in all things (1 Tim 3:11); younger widows should remarry and not be enrolled as official widows of the community (1 Tim 5:9, 11); women are especially susceptible to heresy (2 Tim 3:6–7); older women should teach younger women to be submissive to their husbands (Titus 2:3–5).[45] With

---

[45] On women in the Pastoral Epistles, see esp. Else Kähler, *Die Frau in den paulinischen Briefen* (Zurich: Gotthelf, 1960) 141–71; Hans-Werner Bartsch, *Die Anfänge urchristlicher Rechtsbildungen: Studien zu den Pastoralbriefen* (Theologische Forschung

the exception of the possible existence of the office of deacon for women, each of these items points toward restrictions, limitations, subordination for women. From this, one would have the impression that an increasing emphasis on the subordination of women characterized the early church.

If we contrast this picture with a writing emerging from another group which sees itself in the Pauline tradition, the *Acts of Paul and Thecla*,[46] it becomes clear that this was not the case. This work, not included in our canon but nevertheless translated into many languages, enjoying wide popularity for centuries, is the story of a young woman who left family and fiancé to follow Paul. Twice sentenced to die, once for the crime of abandoning her fiancé and once for defending herself against rape, Thecla was saved by miraculous means. She baptized herself in the face of death, was rescued from death and later donned men's clothing and set out in search of Paul. When Thecla found Paul, he told her, "Go and teach the word of God." The work ends with, "after enlightening many with the word of God, she slept a noble sleep."

Concerning women, the *Acts of Paul and Thecla* is nearly diametrically opposed to the Pastoral Epistles. Whereas the former offers women celibacy as an alternative to marriage, the Pastorals insist that women enter into patriarchal marriage. Whereas the women addressed by the Pastorals are told that salvation will come through childbearing, Thecla is neither mother nor bride. Whereas the Pastorals attempt to limit the office of widow to older women and insist that women learn in silence and not teach, the *Acts of Paul and Thecla* approvingly depicts Thecla as evangelizing.

These two writings represent a solution to the ambiguity in Paul. The *Acts of Paul and Thecla* represents a continuation of Paul's preference for celibacy (1 Cor 7:8–9, 39–40), his collegiality with women and his view that gender distinctions are no longer relevant in Christ. The

---

34; Hamburg: Reich/Evangelischer, 1965) 60–81; Otto Bangerter, *Frauen im Aufbruch: Die Geschichte einer Frauenbewegung in der Alten Kirche* (Neukirchen-Vluyn: Neukirchener Verlag, 1971) 39–64; Gerhard Lohfink, "Weibliche Diakone im Neuen Testament?" *Diakonia* 11 (1980) 385–400. For a discussion of early Christian widowhood in the context of ancient society, see Jo Ann McNamara, "Wives and Widows in Early Christian Thought," *International Journal of Women's Studies* 2 (1979) 575–92.

[46] Translation in *New Testament Apocrypha* (ed. E. Hennecke and W. Schneemelcher; 2 vols.; Philadelphia: Westminster, 1965) 2. 353–64. See Dennis MacDonald, "Virgins, Widows, and Paul in Second Century Asia Minor," *Society of Biblical Literature 1979 Seminar Papers* 1. 169–84; Stevan L. Davies, *The Revolt of the Widows: The Social World of the Apocryphal Acts* (Carbondale, IL: Southern Illinois University, 1980); E. Margaret Howe, "Interpretations of Paul in the Acts of Paul and Thecla," in *Pauline Studies: Essays Presented to Professor F. F. Bruce on his 70th Birthday* (ed. Donald A. Hagner and Murray J. Harris; Grand Rapids, MI: Eerdmans, 1980) 33–49; Ross S. Kraemer, "The Conversion of Women to Ascetic Forms of Christianity," *Signs* 6 (1980) 298–307; Dennis R. MacDonald, *The Legend and the Apostle: The Battle for Paul in Story and Canon* (Philadelphia: Westminster, 1983).

Pastorals represent a clear break with Paul's preference for celibacy, but are in continuity with his conservative views on social customs and women and with his rationale for these (1 Cor 11:2–16). If 1 Cor 14:34–36 is by Paul, this would be a further point of continuity.

From the Pastorals and the *Acts of Paul and Thecla* we can see that there were at least two ways of thinking about women in communities that appealed to Paul as an authority. (Colossians and Ephesians are not necessarily to be subsumed under the line of the Pastorals.) The communities that gave rise to and passed on these works were apparently engaged in debate concerning what was appropriate behavior for women. What role women played in these debates is difficult to reconstruct. Perhaps the widows in the community(-ies) of the Pastorals were among the leadership of the opposition, for the author goes to some lengths to try to limit their authority and church activities (1 Tim 5:3–16). That there were women in the opposition is clear in any case from 2 Tim 3:6. As for the *Acts of Paul and Thecla*, while it is not a model of feminist thinking, the figure of Thecla did offer women an alternative to patriarchal marriage,[47] namely celibacy, and she did serve as a model for women performing missionary activity. Tertullian attests that women in late second- or early third-century Carthage appealed to Thecla as a justification for their own right to baptize (*De bapt.* 17). Thecla was also a model for ascetic women in the fourth century.[48] The document was probably an especially effective instrument in the church's mission to women. Even this brief outline of the development of two streams of early Christian thought demonstrates the necessity of including extra-canonical sources. It reminds us that the author of the Pastoral Epistles probably had to reckon with opposition from women within the communities addressed and gives us a much more balanced picture of the historical development.

IV. *Restructuring Requires Employing New Sources*

It should be obvious that if our goal is to hear women, then writings by women should take top priority.[49] On the early Christian side, the

---

[47] On virginity as freedom from submission to a husband, see Cyprian *De habitu virg.* 22 (CSEL 3,1, p. 203); Leander of Seville *De institut. virg.*, preface (*PL* 72.880A).

[48] See, e.g., Gregory of Nyssa *Vita Macrinae* 2 (SC 178.146); Ambrose *De virg.* 2,3 (*PL* 16.223-24).

[49] A good selection of the writings of the Greek poets Sappho, Corinna, Erinna, Anyte, Nossis and of the Roman poet Sulpicia can be found in Lefkowitz and Fant, *Women's Life*, 3–10, 131–32. Goodwater (*Women*) has bibliographic sections on each of the ancient women authors. On Sappho, see esp. Judith P. Hallett, "Sappho and Her Social Context: Sense and Sensuality," *Signs* 4 (1979) 447–64; Eva Stehle Stigers, "Romantic Sensuality, Poetic Sense: A Response to Hallett on Sappho," *Signs* 4 (1979) 465–71; Page DuBois, "Sappho and Helen," in *Women in the Ancient World*, 95–105.

recent collection, *A Lost Tradition*,[50] provides an easily accessible translation of *The Martyrdom of Perpetua*,[51] the Vergilian Cento of *Faltonia Proba Bona*,[52] the *Pilgrimage of Egeria*[53] and the *Eulogy* of Eudoxia. Also important are such oral traditions of early Christian women as the sayings of Maximilla and Priscilla[54] and the sayings of the Desert Mothers.[55] Of further interest is a work such as the *Acts of Paul and Thecla*, which, whether women were involved in the composition at any stage or not, probably was directed toward women and did, in any case, find popularity among women.

Nonliterary documents form another category of sources which has been hitherto overlooked. Of special importance here are papyrus letters written by women; these are both business and private letters. Also relevant are such legal documents as marriage, wet-nurse, and loan contracts, tax receipts and bills of sale in which women play a role. There has been nearly no systematic study of these documents to date, the work of Sarah Pomeroy[56] and Alanna Emmett[57] forming the notable exceptions. Another category of nonliterary documents that deserves greater attention is inscriptions. Susan Treggiari's study of slave women mentioned in inscriptions demonstrates how fruitful such work could be.[58] Within Judaism, titles of synagogue leadership for women found in Greek and Latin inscriptions represent evidence for a phenomenon not

---

[50] Patricia Wilson-Kastner et al., *A Lost Tradition: Women Writers of the Early Church* (Washington, DC: University Press of America, 1981).

[51] See also the bilingual edition by Herbert Musurillo, *The Acts of the Christian Martyrs* (Oxford: Clarendon, 1972) 106–31.

[52] See also the bilingual edition and commentary by Elizabeth A. Clark and Diane F. Hatch, *The Golden Bough, the Oaken Cross: The Virgilian Cento of Faltonia Betitia Proba* (AAR Texts and Translations 5; Chico, CA: Scholars Press, 1981).

[53] See also the recent German translation and commentary by Herbert Donner, *Pilgerfahrt ins Heilige Land: Die ältesten Berichte christlicher Palästinapilger (4.-7. Jahrhundert)* (Stuttgart: Katholisches Bibelwerk, 1979) 69–137.

[54] Collected in Hennecke and Schneemelcher, *New Testament Apocrypha*, 2. 687.

[55] Included among the *Apophthegmata Patrum* (PG 65.201–4 [Theodora], 419–22 [Sara], 421–28 [Synklētikē]).

[56] Pomeroy is at present doing a comprehensive study of women in Ptolemaic Egypt which is based primarily upon the papyri. See also her "Women in Roman Egypt. A preliminary study based on papyri," in *Reflections of Women in Antiquity* (ed. H. P. Foley; New York: Gordon and Breach, 1982) 303–22.

[57] Alanna Emmett is a member of the team editing the *Corpus Papyrorum Christianarum* at Macquarie University in North Ryde, NSW, Australia. In her work, she is focusing on papyrus sources for early Christian women's monasticism.

[58] Susan Treggiari, "Jobs in the Household of Livia," *Papers of the British School at Rome* 43 (1975) 48–77; idem, "Jobs for Women," *American Journal of Ancient History* 1 (1976) 76–104; idem, "Questions on Women Domestics in the Roman West," in *Schiavitù, manomissione e classi dipendenti nel mondo antico* (Università degli studi di Padova pubblicazioni dell' istituto di storia antica 13; Padua: Istituto di storia antica, 1979) 185–201; idem, "Contubernales in CIL 6," *Phoenix* 35 (1981) 42–69.

otherwise known to us from ancient Jewish literature.[59] Donative and cultic inscriptions mentioning women, as well as inscriptions in which women's civic titles occur, are also especially important.[60] Papyrus documents and inscriptions are in one sense the only primary written sources from antiquity. Any literature that has been copied and recopied has also been susceptible to redaction, censorship, selective compilation, canonization, etc. The community handing down the literature has exerted control over it and formed it. Whether, on the other hand, nonliterary sources survive is usually a matter of climate and historical accident, which means that for the most part, what we do have is both untampered with and probably a better cross-section of what originally existed. Further, nonliterary documents are, by nature of the subjects they treat, probably closer to women's daily life in antiquity than is ancient literature. Systematic work that takes into account the qualitative differences between literary and nonliterary materials could produce new insights into women's lives in antiquity.

A further source of new information concerning women could be monumental remains. Archaeological remains afford an enormous opportunity: they are without male bias. Objects and rooms used by women are as likely to have survived as those used by men. Here the present problem is really not with the ancient evidence but rather with modern interpreters of it. A good example of this is the question of a women's gallery or section in the ancient synagogue.[61] In the ancient synagogue remains themselves there is no evidence that women sat separately from men, such as donative inscriptions honoring those who built, furnished, or decorated a women's gallery or section or inscriptions in the mosaic floor indicating where women and men were to sit. If one were to examine only the synagogue remains, the question of a women's section would not even arise. Nor would ancient literature lead us to a women's gallery or section, for the Jewish and non-Jewish sources of the period do not make mention of a women's gallery or women's section in the synagogue. The origin of the reconstruction is contemporary Orthodox practice, which certainly extends back in time, but we do not know how far back. There is in any case no firm evidence that an architectural divider separated the women from the men. If that is the case, then the prevailing image of women and synagogue services in antiquity requires revision. It is no longer impossible to imagine that women could have served in liturgical functions or in an administrative capacity. This example

[59] See Brooten, *Women Leaders*, 1–99, pls. I–X, 223–50.

[60] See, e.g., Ramsay MacMullen, "Woman in Public in the Roman Empire," *Historia. Zeitschrift für Alte Geschichte* 29 (1980) 208–18.

[61] See Brooten, *Women Leaders*, 103–38, pls. XI–LIII, 250–61.

indicates the potential gain for women's history that studying monumental remains could have. Another especially promising area of research seems to me to be private homes, with an eye toward spaces used primarily or only by women. How often and in which periods and regions do we find evidence for a *gynaikeia*, that is, separate sleeping and living(?) quarters for women? Are there class differences with respect to its existence? Where is it located within the house? How often does one find evidence that women worked in the *gynaikeia* (e.g., spindle whorls or other textile equipment)? Clarification of these questions could shed light on early Christian women's sexuality; on the work of women missionaries to women, whose locus of activity was apparently the women's quarters of households; and on the question of the seclusion of virgins, especially in Judaism and Christianity.

Archaeological research could also be especially important for the study of women and work in antiquity. Here again, women's tools are no less extant than men's tools. Spinning equipment and cooking tools exist side by side with hunting equipment or weapons, and yet there has been a marked tendency on the part of archaeologists to display greater interest in the latter than the former. Agriculture represents an ambivalent area. The general assumption has been that only or mainly men were involved in agriculture, but this may not be the case. A careful examination of pictorial evidence and of literary sources may lead us to the conclusion that women were also involved in agriculture or in some types of agriculture, which would mean that some of the extant farm tools were used by women. Archaeology could also shed light on other questions of women and work. It would be helpful to know, for example, in what kind of physical surroundings the Lydia of Acts 16:14–15, 40 sold her purple; where she purchased it; and which other types of merchants would have worked in her vicinity.

Pictorial evidence, statues, and terra-cottas could lead to new insights in a number of areas. Erotic art could help us to understand women's sexuality better (or male attitudes toward women's and men's sexuality). One could learn more about women's work and daily activities through pictorial depictions, and paintings and statues are the best guide we have to women's hairstyles and clothing. The latter items are of theological significance for early Christianity (e.g., 1 Cor 11:2–16; 1 Tim 2:9–10; Tertullian, *On the Veiling of Virgins*), and Jewish sources also devote some attention to the veiling of women. Perhaps a thorough survey of depictions of women could help to clarify what type of veil the Jewish and Christian sources presuppose. Women's cultic activities occasionally occur in paintings and reliefs, but one must be cautious in interpreting mythic scenes as actually cultic. A more thorough study of women in Christian catacomb paintings could be relevant here, and another fruitful area would be the depiction of women saints in early

Christian art. The Thecla images, for example, often with cropped or flowing hair, are evidence of a different model for women than the usually veiled and demure virgin Mary of the Middle Ages or the modern period.[62]

In addition to these sources, future research will also likely employ the traditional male sources in a new way. Hagiographical materials, for example, or biographies of holy women, if studied critically and with the question of how they might have related to women's history and piety, could be very useful sources. Prescriptive literature studied together with legal and economic documents could also yield new insights. In sum, although scarcity of sources is a problem, lack of ancient evidence is not the reason for our knowing at present so little about early Christian women's history.

Summary

One who takes up the task of early Christian women's history discovers that the present framework of study is not suited to that task. Scholars at present study early Christian women within a framework that is asymmetrical, comparing woman in early Christianity with woman in ancient Judaism and with woman in the Greek and Roman worlds. The present division of disciplines is based on criteria not appropriate to the study of woman, thereby leading to the study of woman as a literary motif or to women being used to prove the superiority of Christianity over Judaism. The limitation to normative canons of literature is similarly questionable. Placing women at the center of the study will mean cutting through the disciplines and being comprehensive with respect to literary sources. It will result in a different view of the relationship between religion and culture and between theology and society. If women are no longer relegated to the cultural background or the societal context, but are recognized as central for understanding early Christianity and its theology, a rethinking of the whole will be required. This will not mean a harmonious complementarity of women's history and men's history, simply adding the two together, thereby leaving the structures of male history and theology intact. Rather, early Christian women's history, as prehistory, that is, as qualitatively different from the history of early Christian men, demonstrates the fragmentary and perspectival nature of what has passed as early Christian history. Thus, the goal of writing early Christian women's history is that it result in a new view of women and in a new view of men.

---

[62] See Claudia Nauerth and Rüdiger Warns, *Thekla: Ihre Bilder in der frühchristlichen Kunst* (Göttinger Orientforschungen. II. Reihe: Studien zur spätantiken und frühchristlichen Kunst 3; Wiesbaden: Harrassowitz, 1981).

5

THE FEMINIST AND THE BIBLE: HERMENEUTICAL ALTERNATIVES

Carolyn Osiek

Literature on feminist method is growing at such a pace that it has rather quickly become an extended field of inquiry in itself, of which the present volume is adequate testimony. It is not the purpose of this chapter to attempt a documented history of the feminist movement as it deals with biblical literature. For that reason whatever documentation is given is intended to be not exhaustive but representative. Rather, the intent of the present essay is to explore some of the ways in which feminists, in particular feminist biblical scholars, are meeting the challenge of adequately and sensitively interpreting biblical texts and the biblical tradition in the light of experience. Nor is it my intention to attribute superiority or inferiority to any one, but rather to "objectively" describe and interpret each, bearing in mind of course the axiom of contemporary hermeneuticists that no interpretation is purely objective but is always conditioned by the presuppositions and prejudices of the interpreter.

With that in mind, it would probably be no waste of paper to briefly set out the presuppositions and prejudices that I consciously bring to the undertaking. The careful reader will no doubt detect others of which I am not aware. Thus the interpretive process goes on. First, I belong to a large institutional church with an amazing amount of diversity in its membership and a firmly entrenched patriarchal leadership. Although that should not determine the direction of my critical scholarship, it inevitably affects my experience; and the two cannot be totally separated. Second, I take note that the very fact that we spend so much time and energy wrestling with biblical texts and traditions, the very fact that there is such a thing as "biblical scholarship," means whether we care to acknowledge it or not that the Bible is more for us than a curious piece of history. It is part of our own *living* history, a power to be reckoned with in the communities of faith to which we belong or from which our students and friends come. Even those who assume a rejectionist stance toward the Bible admit by their position that there is not much middle ground; indifference to the Bible is a difficult path for the serious student of Christianity to tread.

Third, I judge as the result of my own investigation and reflection that it is unnecessary to throw out the baby with the bathwater. The biblical tradition contains enough of lasting and universal value that it is worth salvaging, in spite of the tremendous problems entailed in the salvage operation. Fourth, issues such as authority, inerrancy, revelation, and inspiration must be handled with careful nuances, their theoretical frameworks constructed not in the abstract but in constant interplay with the lived experience of whole communities of faith. Finally, it is my conviction that the illusive entity that we call "tradition" is the all-encompassing movement that contains within itself the biblical text and the factors leading to its production. It contains as well the reflective interpretation of that articulation in subsequent generations, including our own, as persons in concretized life situations bring the text to bear on their own experience and, no less important, their experience to bear on the text. In other words, tradition is not a boundary but an open road that connects us with the past and points us in the direction of the future.

A discussion of feminist alternatives in biblical interpretation cannot be undertaken in isolation from either recent currents in feminism or in biblical interpretation; hence a few summary remarks about both by way of establishing a context for what follows. Rosemary Ruether has admirably summed up the three major directions in contemporary feminism as liberal, socialist/Marxist, and romantic/radical.[1]

Liberal feminism takes the model of progress within a capitalist society and works for political reform, equal rights, and improved working conditions, with the assumption that the present social and economic system of Western countries is still redeemable and reformable. It thus carries within it the tendency to classism, to the identification of the rights of upper-middle-class white women with "women's rights," to the neglect of the plight, interests, and needs of women who are caught in the economically oppressive web of the working classes, minorities, and the poor. Much of the accusation that has been leveled against the feminist movement by working and minority women has identified feminism with this "liberal feminism," which seems to have little to offer them. It is an indictment of the middle-class feminists of recent years for their failure to see beyond their own horizons.

Socialist or Marxist feminism according to Ruether follows upon the Marxist assumption that full equality can be achieved only by the full integration of labor and ownership; thus only by the complete assimilation of women into the work force, which is at the same time in control

---

[1] R. Ruether, *Sexism and God-Talk: Toward a Feminist Theology* (Boston: Beacon, 1983) 41–45, 216–32.

of the means of production, can the exploitation of women cease. In the socialist experiences that have so far been tried, however, such has not been the case, because the patriarchal structure of the family has not given way to an egalitarian one commensurate with the political philosophy upon which the public sphere is based. Hence women in socialist societies find themselves under the double burden of making a full contribution in the work force while continuing to be the major source of domestic labor. The only apparent way out of this dilemma is to restructure completely the reproductive and preservative functions of human society in other ways than that of the traditional family, an extreme to which few societies are willing to go.

If liberal and socialist feminism assume that the way to equality is through full participation of women in the public sphere, in what has traditionally been the male world, romantic feminism does just the opposite. It exults in the differences between men and women, upholds the feminine way as innately superior, and glorifies the so-called feminine qualities of sensitivity, creativity, intuition, bodiliness, etc. as the true female self that the predominant rational, hierarchical, exploitative masculine society consistently tries to repress by patriarchal domination. The reformist branch of romantic feminism sees as its mission the transformation of the morally and aesthetically inferior masculine world through infusion of superior feminine values. The radical branch of romantic feminism proclaims the necessity of total withdrawal from the male world in a separatist stance that will be ultimately the only way to save women for themselves. In either case the resulting end product is simply a reversal of the domination and alienation that are seen to be the major problems within a patriarchal structure. The oppressed will become the oppressors, and no advance toward mutuality will be realized.

In Ruether's schema, a liberation-hermeneutical feminism would represent a fourth type of feminism, which attempts to incorporate the best elements of the other three: the concern for human development and societal egalitarianism of liberal feminism, the social critique and dedication to building a just society of socialist feminism, and the sensitivity to deeper human values of romantic feminism. A true liberation feminism would thus be able to transcend the limits of the other three types. Its focus on the experience of the oppressed would free it from the bourgeois complacency to which liberal feminism is prone. Its vision of a new society would abolish the patriarchalism which socialist feminism has not succeeded in eliminating. Finally, a true liberation feminism would struggle for the liberation not only of women but of all human persons in a community of mutuality in which neither mode of being, "masculine" or "feminine," consistently dominates. It is this liberation hermeneutic which makes the strongest claim for biblical grounding, and, as we shall see below, this may be one of its most problematic aspects.

Because we are part of our recent history, because we are involved in the process of creating that history, and because any contemporary hermeneutic must be as deeply grounded in experience as it is in theory, these alternatives in the feminist movement at large provide the basic categories within which biblical feminists also operate, whether we are aware of it or not. While not fitting neatly within the same slots, feminist biblical interpretation raises very similar questions and faces many of the same dilemmas, as we shall see below. Contemporary critical feminism attempts to confront and address the problems inherent in all four of the approaches outlined above.

If critical feminism is at the point of breaking through an impasse into a new consciousness ready to try new alternatives, the same can be said of contemporary biblical method. After nearly a century of domination by the historical-critical method, its limits and inherent prejudices are becoming widely accepted. Although the method itself will continue to hold an important and fundamental place in biblical studies for the foreseeable future, it can no longer be *the* method, the criterion to which all interpretation must be submitted. Current biblical studies demonstrate a diversity of methods, some new, some of long duration with only minimal recognition: literary criticism, structuralism, social and sociological interpretation, and the various forms of spiritual and psychological interpretation are all adapted from other disciplines, thus giving evidence of the growing awareness that biblical interpretation cannot function in isolation from the social and intellectual world of the interpreter, a world that is too pluriform and complex to be served only within the limited boundaries of historical-critical exegesis. Just as the varieties of feminist critique challenge traditional patriarchy, so too the varieties of biblical method challenge traditional exegesis and demonstrate that its claim to be "value-free" is simply false.

Others have previously undertaken the task of examining the various methods for approaching biblical material about women with a view to integrating it into a relevant contemporary hermeneutic. For example, K. Sakenfeld in 1981 summarized the alternatives as the following: (1) focusing on texts that portray women in a positive way to counteract the devastatingly negative texts "against" women; (2) rejecting the Bible altogether as "not authoritative and/or useful"; (3) looking more broadly to biblical texts that lend themselves to a liberation perspective; (4) taking a culturally comparative approach to analyze "the intersection of the stories of ancient and modern women living in patriarchal culture."[2] To

---

[2] Katherine Doob Sakenfeld, "Response to Rosemary Radford Ruether's 'Christology and Feminism: Can a Male Savior Help Women?'" unpublished paper for the AAR Feminist Hermeneutic Project, Liberation Theology Working Group, April 1981, as summarized in Letty M. Russell, "In Search of a Critical Feminist Paradigm for Biblical Interpretation," unpublished paper for the same Working Group, April, 1983, p. 2.

these alternatives could be added a fifth: standing back from the specific focus on women as in (3) above, but concentrating on the broader issue of inclusive biblical anthropology.[3]

Essentially the five options listed above can be reduced to three: focus on women (1) and (4); situate women within a broader context (3) and (5); give up on the Bible altogether as hopeless (2). Teaching and research on women in the Bible in recent years has played on all five. In the following remarks I would like to suggest yet another way of examining the alternatives for feminist biblical hermeneutics, one that I believe is thematically more inclusive and deals with all options previously discussed. Some may question use of the word "feminist" for some of these alternatives, but the term is to be taken here in its broadest sense, as concern for the promotion and dignity of women in all aspects of society, and in this context especially inasmuch as that promotion and dignity are conditioned by biblical interpretation. Some too may question the appropriateness of "hermeneutic" as a classification in some cases. Again, I am taking the term in its broadest sense, as a principle of interpretation, while still confining it to interaction with biblical data. Others may consider that one or other of what are proposed here are hardly acceptable as alternatives or options, either within the range of what is life-giving to women or within the limits of possible responses that would remain true to theological premises or contemporary assumptions. I would argue that such judgments are subjective and that as long as a significant number of women in or on the margins of the Western Christian tradition find one or other of these alternatives to be their way of functioning meaningfully within their context—as indeed they do in every case—it is a valid alternative for those who would take it. Bear in mind once again that what follows is description, not advocacy. (These considerations are deliberately limited to the Christian experience in the West, since I do not claim sufficient knowledge of other religious traditions. I leave it to those who do to respond out of their own experience.)

The question proposed then is: When women today in Christian communities become aware of their situation within a patriarchal religious institution, and, moreover, when they recognize that the Bible is a major implement for maintaining the oppression of the patriarchal structure, what are the ways in which they respond and adjust to that situation? I suggest that there are five ways: rejectionist, loyalist, revisionist, sublimationist, and liberationist.

The rejectionist alternative is familiar enough in the recent past. It resembles Sakenfeld's second method, rejecting the Bible as not authoritative or useful, though some rejectionist writers go further, to the total

---

[3] As explored in Adela Yarbro Collins, "An Inclusive Biblical Anthropology," *Theology Today* 34 (1978) 358–69.

rejection not only of the Bible but of the whole religious tradition it represents. Seen from this perspective, the entire Judeo-Christian tradition is hopelessly sinful, corrupt, and unredeemable. The long-discussed hermeneutical question whether patriarchy is a separable attribute in Judaism and Christianity, from which it could be purged, or whether patriarchalism is an inherent characteristic inseparable from its nature is answered with the latter: because patriarchalism is an essential and corrupt component of Judaism-Christianity, the whole religious tradition must be rejected.

Beginnings of this position can be seen as early as Elizabeth Cady Stanton, who refused to be present at a suffragist prayer meeting at which the opening hymn was "Guide Us, O Thou Great Jehovah," on the principle that Jehovah had "never taken any active part in the suffrage movement."[4] Yet her great project of *The Woman's Bible* clearly shows that ninety years ago even she was not prepared to reject the whole of her religious tradition, perhaps because she saw too well that she would win more converts by remaining in the struggle.

The primary proponent of the rejectionist alternative today is of course Mary Daly, whose writings on the subject are well known.[5] For Daly, the only acceptable hermeneutical principle is that of the remnant of women who leave the unsavable Judeo-Christian legacy perpetrated by men and together form a new post-Christian faith capable of conquering the evil of patriarchalism and transcending its negative power. Ultimately this direction leads to a new dualism, in which maleness symbolizes evil and femaleness good, a reversal of the ancient Platonic cosmic/symbolic hierarchy, but a hierarchy nevertheless.[6]

The rejectionist hermeneutic is the most extreme theological form of radical separatism. Carried out faithfully in the social, economic, and political spheres, it would be not only very difficult but also very disruptive if successful. Even as a biblical hermeneutic, its implications are quite serious. It not only rejects what is proclaimed to be a major redemptive vehicle of Judaism and Christianity as nonredemptive; but it also rejects the possibility of conversion for its entire structure and its supporters. There is a kind of extreme apocalyptic finalism, rigid and unbending, which cannot yield to a dynamic of conversion. This indicates its major weakness: an almost total rootlessness from the historical

---

[4] Quoted in Elisabeth Schüssler Fiorenza, *In Memory of Her: A Feminist Theological Reconstruction of Christian Origins* (New York: Crossroad, 1983), 7.

[5] Principally *Beyond God the Father: Toward a Philosophy of Women's Liberation* (Boston: Beacon, 1973) and *Gyn/Ecology: The Metaethics of Radical Feminism* (Boston: Beacon, 1979).

[6] See R. Ruether's brilliant description of Daly's theology as neo-Gnosticism, "now built on the dualism of a transcendent spirit world of femaleness over against the deceitful anticosmos of masculinity," *Sexism and God-Talk*, 230 and 284 n. 16.

past and from much of the historical and social present. Its only roots are in a hypothetical prehistoric past of idyllic goddess worship and a projected eschatological future in which evil (male) will be overcome by good (female).

The second hermeneutical alternative is the loyalist one, in most ways the opposite of the rejectionist. There the foundational premise is the essential validity and goodness of the biblical tradition as Word of God, which cannot be dismissed under any circumstance. The biblical witness as revelation has an independent status which need not be vindicated by human authority: the Bible is the ultimate expression of God's authority, not only descriptive but prescriptive, to which all human inquiry must submit. Yet the Bible, precisely as Word of God, cannot by nature be oppressive. If it is seen to be so, then the mistake lies with the interpreter and interpretive tradition, not with the text. It is the interpreter who is sinful, not the content; the medium which is found wanting, not the message. Biblical revelation is intended to foster the greatest human happiness for all, but such happiness may not always conform to the standards of contemporary culture. The Bible proclaims a message of true freedom and humanization, but according to a divine plan, not a human one. Men and women are intended to live in true happiness and mutual respect within that divine plan, not in oppressive patterns of domination and struggle against one another, which are sinful manifestations of the disorder of human nature without divine grace.

As long as one is dealing with general principles of religious anthropology and virtuous living, such premises pose little problem. But how are these hermeneutical principles to be reconciled with the blatant biblical message of female submission, especially in the household codes of the New Testament? Herein lies the problem. Two somewhat different kinds of responses are offered within this alternative. The first is to employ careful critical exegesis to counter one text with another in order to refute simplistic literalist interpretations of any one passage: for example, 1 Cor 14:34 with 11:5, 1 Tim 2:12 with Titus 2:3, etc. By building a carefully constructed argument step by step, totally based on thorough and sound exegesis of actual passages, this approach can demonstrate to the mind that is a priori open to expanding roles of women, but unyielding on the precise definition of biblical authority and revelation, that contrary to conclusions reached by a superficial reading of the texts, the Bible may not at all be condemning women to an inferior position. The problem has been with closed-minded interpreters, not with the text itself.[7] Thus the new exposition calls for conversion of social attitudes to

---

[7] Examples of this kind of hermeneutic are Richard and Joyce Boldrey, *Chauvinist or Feminist? Paul's View of Women* (Grand Rapids: Baker, 1976); Evelyn and Frank Stagg, *Woman in the World of Jesus* (Philadelphia: Westminster, 1978).

the true biblical spirit of mutual respect.

The second form taken by the loyalist hermeneutic is to accept the traditional argument for order through hierarchy as a datum of revelation but one sorely in need of transformation from within because of its abuse by imperfect human instruments. Thus it is argued that the subordination theme applies only or chiefly to the family, not to society at large, and is totally misunderstood and abused when seen as dominance/ submission. Rather the point is the necessary leadership of one and followership of the other as the only and divinely intended way to unity and harmony in society. Far from diminishing the dignity and freedom of women, such a structure adhered to with love promotes the true liberation of both women and men to fulfill their divinely intended destiny.[8]

Those who might tend to dismiss the loyalist hermeneutic too easily should recall that it is a carefully worked out biblical method, usually based on sound use of exegetical method, and that it is found useful by large numbers of intelligent American women as a means of explaining and interpreting their role within their biblical faith. It is an acceptable way of using contemporary exegetical method within a conservative theological structure and is an excellent demonstration that it is not exegesis that will finally determine how one interprets biblical data, but experiential and theological premises. This fact indicates too the chief weaknesses of the loyalist method: it is particularly vulnerable to the temptation to stretch history and the literal meaning of texts, and it tends to be innocent of the political implications of the types of social interaction and relationships that it advocates on the basis of fidelity to the biblical text as divine revelation.

If the rejectionist hermeneutic holds the biblical tradition as unconvertible and the loyalist hermeneutic holds it as not in need of conversion, the third alternative, a revisionist hermeneutic, represents a midpoint between the two. The foundational premise of this hermeneutic is that the patriarchal mold in which the Judeo-Christian tradition has been cast is historically but not theologically determined. Because of social and historical factors the tradition has been male-dominated, androcentric, and discriminatory, but these characteristics are separable from and thus not intrinsic to it. The tradition is capable of being reformed, the perspective revised—and that is precisely the religious challenge addressed to the contemporary feminist.

The method is research into women's history to reveal neglected sources of information in the tradition. In this approach, which combines Sakenfeld's (1) and (4), the historical sources are reexamined and reinterpreted to show how much we really do know about women and their

---

[8] An example of this approach is Susan T. Foh, *Women and the Word of God: A Response to Biblical Feminism* (Grand Rapids: Baker, 1979).

contributions to the formation of history. For example, the role of women in the Jewish scriptures and the Talmud is interpreted against the backdrop of whatever information is available from archaeological and artistic sources; the role of women in the New Testament and early church is interpreted from the portrayal of women in the gospels, the Pauline mission, the apocryphal acts, the martyrdom literature, etc. The historical sense of "reading between the lines" is employed to portray the positive role of women in ancient sources. Meanwhile, the chauvinist-misogynist texts are explained by a combination of exegetical method and interpretation of the influence of cultural context. This approach has produced a long list of books in the last ten years on the role of women in Judaism and early Christianity and the ministry of women in the early church, so numerous that it is unnecessary to give examples. It has also produced a few fine literary studies that have reexamined familiar texts with the tools of literary criticism to reveal the androcentric one-sidedness of traditional interpretation.[9]

The revisionist alternative adopts the position that the tradition is worth saving, and it has thus become the starting point for many feminist religious thinkers with liberal theologies of revelation who are not willing to abandon the tradition entirely as do the rejectionists. It takes the tactic of highlighting the importance of women in our religious history, of portraying their dignity within patriarchy. It moves ultimately—but not fast enough or firmly enough for some—toward the rehabilitation of the tradition through reform. It proclaims in a moderate voice that the situation cannot long remain the same, but that real change is imperative. Its major weakness is that it attacks more the symptoms than the cause of the illness. It musters no direct frontal attack on the system that has caused the suppression of the very evidence which it painstakingly reconstructs. Its subsequent lack of political strategy undermines its efforts in the short run, though for those with historical patience and vision it probably produces some long-lasting results.

The fourth alternative hermeneutic, the sublimationist, includes some aspects of Ruether's classification of "romantic" feminism, in varying degrees of separatism. Its basic premise is the otherness of the feminine as manifested especially in feminine imagery and symbolism in human culture. As Other, the feminine operates by its own principles and rules, which are totally distinct from those of the male realm. In some versions the feminine is innately superior to the masculine, and therefore any thought of equality or egalitarianism is unthinkable; in other versions the two poles are so different that no comparisons can be

---

[9] The outstanding example is Phyllis Trible, *God and the Rhetoric of Sexuality* (Overtures to Biblical Theology; Philadelphia: Fortress, 1978). See also George H. Tavard, *Woman in Christian Tradition* (Notre Dame, IN: University of Notre Dame Press, 1973).

made, and social equality is simply a nonissue. The life-giving and
nurturing qualities of woman are of a totally different order than the
initiative and constructive qualities of man, and any substantial crossing
over in sex roles is against nature.

In biblical studies the sublimationist hermeneutic takes the form of
the search for and glorification of the eternal feminine in biblical symbolism. Israel as virgin and bride of God, the church as bride of Christ
and mother of the faithful, Mary as virgin-mother who symbolizes Israel,
the church, and the feminine mystique—these are the symbols upon
which the sublimationist hermeneutic focuses. More recently, feminine
imagery for God and Christ has been an important drawing point: the
Christ-Sophia and maternal imagery applied to Christ in patristic and
Christian apocryphal literature, and the feminine symbolism for the
Holy Spirit, which recurs illusively but persistently in Christian literature
and iconography.[10]

This alternative can identify with much of the mystical tradition of
Judaism and Christianity and with a certain amount of traditional Mari-
ology, inasmuch as it can feel at home with erotic imagery in language of
prayer and divine union. It is also closely associated with one type of
Jungianism, which uses biblical symbols as archetypal assertions of the sta-
bility and rightness of distinctive feminine and masculine modes of being.
Its response to the problems of patriarchy and androcentrism is not to join
battle but by a kind of philosophical idealism to transcend the conflict by
ascribing greater importance to the world of symbols, and to assert that the
way to true freedom will be found only by following their lead.

The sublimationist hermeneutic can provide a helpful way of biblical interpretation for those who are adept at handling symbolism and for
whom romantic feminism provides the key to understanding self and
world. Its chief weaknesses are its tendencies to exclusivism and separatism from the social-political dimension and its inclination toward dog-
matism on the question of female and male social roles.

The fifth form of feminist biblical hermeneutics is the most recent and
the one now attracting the most attention. Liberationist feminism, pio-
neered earlier by Letty Russell and others and now being developed principally by Elisabeth Schüssler Fiorenza and Rosemary Radford Ruether,[11]

---

[10] A recent example of this approach which is restrained, well-researched, and does not
escape into sentimentality is Joan C. Engelsman, *The Feminine Dimension of the Divine*
(Philadelphia: Westminster, 1979). Also helpful is Part One of Leonard Swidler, *Biblical
Affirmations of Woman* (Philadelphia: Westminster, 1979) 21–73. Not to be missed is the
fourteenth-century Bavarian church fresco portraying the Trinity as an old man, a
woman, and a young man, on the cover of Swidler's book.
[11] Besides numerous articles by these and other authors, see especially Letty M. Russell,
Human Liberation in a Feminist Perspective (Philadelphia: Westminster, 1974); E.
Fiorenza, *In Memory of Her*, esp. pp. 26–40; R. Ruether, *New Woman/New Earth:*

takes its starting point from the broader perspective of liberation theology. Its basic premise is a radical reinterpretation of biblical eschatology: the reign of God with its redemption is proclaimed as the task and mission of the believer in the world of the present as well as the hope of full realization in God's future. This beginning of its realization for women means liberation from patriarchal domination so that all human persons can be for each other partners and equals in the common task. The oppression of women is part of the larger pattern of dominance-submission, which includes political, economic, and social as well as theological dimensions: "We cannot split a spiritual, antisocial redemption from the human self as a social being, embedded in sociopolitical and ecological systems"; rather, "socioeconomic humanization is indeed the outward manifestation of redemption."[12]

As a biblical hermeneutic, liberationist feminism proclaims that the central message of the Bible is human liberation, that this is in fact the meaning of salvation. It therefore attempts to "come clean" with bold honesty on the question of exegesis and advocacy. Rather than try to maintain that biblical interpretation can be done objectively and in a value-free framework as the historical-critical school and more recently structuralist and sociological interpreters would claim, liberationist biblical theologians, denying that possibility for any theology or hermeneutic, will openly admit that theirs is an advocacy theology, already committed to certain causes and assumptions before it begins—as are, in fact, any of the other four hermeneutical alternatives discussed above as well.

Ruether finds the core of the biblical message of liberation in the prophetic tradition. The preaching of conversion from unjust social and economic practices is the call to create a just society free from any kind of oppression. Thus the hermeneutical dynamic springs from biblical texts that do not deal specifically with women, and which in fact can be quite androcentric and patriarchal at times. Freed from their own historical and cultural contexts, however, the texts inspire a message of human liberation through the working of justice which today addresses us authoritatively within our own contemporary awareness of oppression.

Fiorenza turns her attention more directly to those texts of the New Testament which transcend androcentric-patriarchal structures to express a new vision of redeemed humanity. For both authors, as for all liberationist feminists, it is not just a question of reinterpreting texts within a patriarchal framework, but of actually approaching them with an alternate vision of salvation and new creation, which will not stop at biblical interpretation but will lead inexorably to transformation of the social order

---

Sexist Ideologies and Human Liberation (New York: Seabury, 1975); idem, *Sexism and God-Talk.*

[12] Ruether, *Sexism and God-Talk,* 215–16.

through both individual and communal, structural conversion. Thus the liberationist alternative does not reject the tradition as unredeemable, but demands a total restructuring of its expression.

For the liberationist, the hermeneutical principle upon which to construct a theology of revelation is quite specific. Stated negatively, "whatever diminishes or denies the full humanity of women must be presumed not to reflect the divine or an authentic relation to the divine . . . or to be the message or work of an authentic redeemer or a community of redemption." Stated positively, "what does promote the full humanity of women is of the Holy, it does reflect true relation to the divine . . . the authentic message of redemption and the mission of redemptive community";[13] "biblical revelation and truth are given only in those texts and interpretive models that transcend critically their patriarchal frameworks and allow for a vision of Christian women as historical and theological subjects and actors."[14]

The liberationist hermeneutic holds much promise for creating a new direction in religious feminism. Its principal weakness lies in its almost partisan position on revelation as discussed above. Such a restrictive basis for a theology of revelation can hardly stand up under heavy scrutiny of theological tradition. It seems to equate "revelatory" with "authoritative" in an almost simplistic way, then to reject as non-revelatory whatever does not fit according to its own narrow criterion. Moreover, in its historical approach to biblical literature, this narrow criterion of revelation leads the liberationist method to eulogize the prophets, Jesus, and sometimes Paul while writing off other, particularly later New Testament, writers who do not meet the liberation criterion, thus forming a new "canon within the canon" on very slim foundations. If the liberationist hermeneutic is to exercise the influence for which it has the potential, this weakness must be addressed.

We have surveyed five alternative responses to the question of feminist biblical hermeneutics. They arise from five different sets of women's experiences and assumptions about the Bible. I believe that they are truly alternatives, that is, within the limits imposed upon us by our experience and human conditioning, we really are free to choose our own hermeneutical direction. The category of conversion directed by liberationist feminists to perpetrators of androcentric patriarchy applies to feminists as well, especially to those who by race and class are caught in the double web of being both oppressed and oppressor.

In biblical times, patriarchy and androcentrism were seen not as sinful but as necessary for maintaining order. With consciousness now raised, the primary hermeneutical task is a redefinition of order in

---

13 Ruether, *Sexism and God-Talk*, 19.
14 Fiorenza, *In Memory of Her*, 30.

human society, a hermeneutic already applied in the case of slavery and currently being applied on the issue of the necessity of deterrence for the preservation of peace. There is no reason to treat the evil of patriarchy any less seriously.

6

HIS STORY VERSUS HER STORY:
MALE GENEALOGY AND FEMALE STRATEGY
IN THE JACOB CYCLE*

Nelly Furman

A text, according to the definition that French semiotician Roland Barthes has given the word, is not a literary work or a portion of it, but its conceptualization, that is to say, a reading. Roland Barthes's concept of textuality is often illustrated by the following two metaphors. In the first, the reader is compared to a musician for whom interpretation is an activity, a personal rendition of an original score. Like the musician, the reader proposes a personal understanding of the meaningful aspects of a literary work. Because it is the perception of the reader which creates the text, its coherence is in the eyes of the reader and not in the intentionality of the author(s), narrator(s), or editor(s). The etymology of the word "text" leads us to the second metaphor used to explain the reading process. The Latin noun *textus* means not only text, passage of scripture, but also texture, tissue, structure, and context; the verb *textere* is translated "to construct," "to compose," "to weave." Thus the text is often described as a fabric, a network, or a web. The reader's interest is focused on the materiality of the literary work, the fabric of its narrativity, in other words the processes by which and through which stories are told and understood. The interlacing of narrative threads, the weaving and wavering of plot, the manner in which a yarn is spun create a substratum of meaning that structures, supports, or undermines our understanding of the story. Insofar as it examines the systems of signs that allow literary communication to take place, textual criticism belongs to the semiotic enterprise. Understood as a semiotic exercise, textual criticism is a reading process that differs substantially in its practice and

---

* My thanks to Marilyn F. Collins for inviting me to read a first version of this paper at the Joint Annual Meeting of the American Academy of Religion and the Society of Biblical Literature in San Francisco in 1981.

presuppositions from classical biblical textual approaches and from traditional notions of formal or textual criticism.[1]

Though any number of narrative, linguistic, or thematic features may be used as heuristic devices for a textual reading, features that describe or refer to interpretation are particularly inviting for the semiotician. Thus, characters that function as interpreters and events that emphasize communicative acts are powerful poles of attraction.[2] In this respect, the seduction scene between Joseph and Potiphar's wife (Genesis 39) beckons the interest of the reader, for it deals with two contrary interpretations of one event, two seemingly antithetical readings. Potiphar's wife gives a willfully misleading explanation, which her husband, nonetheless, believes. They are the first set of narrator-narratee encoded in the text. A differing perception of the same event is suggested by the anonymous biblical narrator and Joseph, both of whom guarantee the existence of another viewpoint.

When Jacob's beloved Joseph was taken to Egypt, he was sold to Potiphar, an Egyptian, an officer of Pharaoh and captain of the guard. Pleased with Joseph, Potiphar makes him overseer of his house. While in Potiphar's employ, Joseph, who, according to the narrator, is handsome, attracts the attention of his master's wife. She tries to seduce him. He rejects her advances and explains his refusal in these terms: "Lo, having me my master has no concern about anything in the house, and he has put everything that he has in my hand; he is not greater in this house than I am; nor has he kept back anything from me except yourself, because you are his wife; how then can I do this great wickedness, and sin against God?" (Gen 39:9–10).[3] However, one day, when Joseph is alone in the house, Potiphar's wife grabs him by his coat and again makes overtures. He runs out of the house leaving the garment behind in her hands. She calls in the men of the household and tells them the following: "See, he has brought among us a Hebrew to insult us; he came in to me to lie with me, and I cried out with a loud voice; and when he heard that I lifted up my voice and cried, he left his garment with me, and fled and got out of the house" (Gen 39:15–16). She later repeats the same story to her husband, and Joseph is imprisoned.

One piece of clothing, two stories. His story versus her story. In this episode, Joseph's piece of attire is the mediating object between divergent desires. Here, one garment suggests a male and a female text, two

---

[1] Roland Barthes, "From Work to Text," in *Textual Strategies: Perspectives in Post-Structuralist Criticism* (ed. Josue Harari; Ithaca, NY: Cornell University Press, 1979) 73–81.

[2] For a discussion of the question of reading and its relation to criticism, see Susan R. Suleiman, "Introduction: Varieties of Audience-Oriented Criticism," in *The Reader in the Text: Essays on Audience and Interpretation* (ed. Susan R. Suleiman and Inge Crosman; Princeton, NJ: Princeton University Press, 1980) 3–45.

[3] All biblical quotes are taken from *The New Oxford Annotated Bible*. Revised Standard Version (New York: Oxford University Press, 1973).

gender-marked readings.

If we were to listen solely to the words of Potiphar's wife, as the servants and her husband do, without the leading comments of the narrator, the abandoned garment would stand for his desire and her refusal. The narrator, however, lets us know that Joseph had on previous occasions rejected her advances and that her story is fictional, a total fabrication. Whereas the garment represents for Joseph his loyalty to his master, for her the garment becomes a means of manipulation, a strategic device for a successful frame-up. The interpretation she proposes for the presence of the garment shows that explanation is a matter of point of view and further suggests that it is neither the truth nor the falsehood of the story that matters, but its plausibility. Her husband believes her story and Joseph is sent to prison. For Joseph, the abandoned garment represents his rejection of Potiphar's wife, and therefore his loyalty to his master, and ultimately his obedience to God. In his study entitled *From Canaan to Egypt*, George W. Coats points out that in the context of Joseph's relation to power, the abandoned garment shows first of all "a kind of human enlightenment, a commitment to a fellow man because he is a fellow who trusts the relationship, commitment to a relationship because only in that relationship does life make sense."[4]

For Joseph, garments do have a special meaning and do suggest a specific bond between men. His father, Jacob, gives him a long robe with sleeves for he "loved Joseph more than any other of his children, because he was the son of his old age" (Gen 37:3). Joseph's brothers become resentful and their jealousy turns to hatred after Joseph reports on them to their father and then recounts his dreams, which, according to them, predict that they will bow to him. When Jacob sends his favorite son to see if the others are doing well in the pastures, Joseph's brothers conspire to kill him. Reuben, the oldest, succeeds in convincing them to spare the boy's life. They strip Joseph of his robe and put him in a pit. Midianite traders passing by rescue the boy from the pit and sell him to Ishmaelites. Upon discovering that Joseph had disappeared from the pit where they had hidden him, the brothers take Joseph's robe, dip it in the blood of a goat and show it to their father. Joseph's bloodied robe stands in lieu of an explanation, and Jacob understandably concludes that his favorite son has been devoured by a wild beast.

Jacob gave Joseph the robe as a token of his affection for him. When Joseph abandons his coat in the hands of Potiphar's wife, his stated reason is his respect for his master. In both cases, a piece of attire represents an emotional link, a trust between men. When the Pharaoh makes

---

[4] George W. Coats, *From Canaan to Egypt: Structural and Theological Context for the Joseph Story* (Catholic Biblical Quarterly Monograph Series 4; Washington, DC: Catholic Biblical Association, 1976) 89.

Joseph vizier of Egypt, he gives the young Hebrew not only his signet ring but also garments of fine linen and a gold chain (Gen 41:42). Joseph will mark his reconciliation with his brothers by giving them ceremonial garments as well as provisions before they leave Egypt (Gen 45:21). For the men, garments express feelings. When overcome with grief, men tear their clothes. Reuben, upon discovering Joseph's disappearance, "rends" his clothes (Gen 37:29), and so does Jacob upon being shown Joseph's bloodied robe (Gen 37:34). Later on, when they are accused of having stolen the divining cup, Joseph's brothers too "rend" their clothes (Gen 44:13). Whether a token of love and respect or a sign of despair and mourning, for Jacob and his sons, garments are symbolic items.

By giving Joseph a long robe with sleeves, Jacob sets Joseph apart from his brothers. Joseph will emulate his father's partiality, for he will give his full brother Benjamin not just one ceremonial vestment, as he gave his other brothers, but "three hundred shekels of silver and five festal garments" (Gen 45:22). By distinguishing among siblings without regard to the order of birth, Jacob sets up a hierarchical order founded on the father's liking for a child, and garments are the distinguishing markers of this new filial order. Joseph's robe establishes a visible link between father and son: the seal of approval for all to see of Joseph's election as favorite son and legitimate heir. Items of clothing are the textual signifiers which, in the latter part of Genesis, support the theme of sibling rivalry and the resulting victory of the youngest. They implement the new hierarchical order of elective dominance in opposition to the "natural" predetermined rule of sovereignty of the first and oldest.

When Rebekah was pregnant with Esau and Jacob, the Lord told her: "Two nations are in your womb, and two peoples, born of you, shall be divided; the one shall be stronger than the other, the elder shall serve the younger" (Gen 25:23). The story of Jacob actualizes the words of the Lord. Esau, the firstborn, "came forth red, all his body like a hairy mantle" (Gen 25:25). Jacob first bought Esau's birthright in exchange for some bread and soup. Then, at the urging of Rebekah, Jacob put on his brother's attire. He covered his hands and neck with the skin of kids fetched so that Rebekah could prepare some savory food for him to bring Isaac. Impersonating his brother, Jacob secured Isaac's blessing meant for Esau.

In *The Art of Biblical Narrative*, Robert Alter reminds us that the midrashic commentators had already noted that the goat and kid established connecting threads between the Judah and Tamar episode and the Joseph story: "The Holy one Praised be He said to Judah, 'You deceived your father with a kid. By your life, Tamar will deceive you with a kid.' . . ."[5] The kids prepared by Rebekah also belong to this network,

[5] Gen 37:31-32; Robert Alter, *The Art of Biblical Narrative* (New York: Basic Books, 1981) 10-11.

and Esau's garment now in Jacob's possession provides us with yet another connecting thread between the stories of Jacob and those of Joseph and Judah. In his article "The Youngest Son or Where does Genesis 38 Belong," Judah Goldin attributes the presence of the Judah and Tamar episode, which is embedded in the story of Joseph, to the thematics of fraternal rivalry.[6] Garments, as we have seen, form the textual support of this theme, and they play as well a prominent role in the story of Judah and Tamar.

Tamar, the widow of Judah's eldest son Er, has remained childless because Onan, Judah's second son "spilled the semen on the ground, lest he should give offspring to his brother" (Gen 38:9). We are told that this displeased God, and Onan too was slain. Judah sends Tamar back to her father's house promising to send his last son Shelah to her when the lad is grown up. Time passes. Judah does not honor his promise. Having learned that Judah, now himself a widower, was going to shear his sheep, Tamar takes off her widow's clothes, puts on a veil and sits by the roadside. Judah mistakes her for a harlot and asks to "come into her" (Gen 38:16). She accepts on the condition that she be given his signet, cord, and staff as a pledge of payment for her favors. This time Judah will be true to his word and send her a kid from his flock, but Tamar having taken off the harlot's veil and dressed in her widow's garment again cannot be found by Judah's envoy. Three months later, Judah learns that his daughter-in-law is pregnant by harlotry. He orders that she be burned, but upon being shown the signet, the cord, and staff which he recognizes as his, Judah declares: "she is more righteous than I, inasmuch as I did not give her my son Shelah" (Gen 38:26).

In the first ruse, Tamar simply exchanges two symbolically marked garments: the widow's clothes, which denote the absence of both husband and sexual relations; a harlot's veil, which advertises readiness for intercourse without parental responsibility. As Onan's punishment suggests and Judah's words confirm, the point of the story is not sexuality but fertility to assure the family's line of descent, a significance which the harlot's veil does not imply. Tamar's second stratagem is shrewder. Like Potiphar's wife, Tamar makes pieces of attire serve her own interest and purpose. The signet, cord, and staff were supposed to be the guarantee of payment Tamar was to receive for her favors. Tamar, however, does not use these objects as promissory notes. For her the importance of the signet, cord, and staff resides neither in their value as objects nor as down payment for a pledge; they are desirable only because they function as signatures, as evidence of the identity of the

---

[6] Judah Goldin, "The Youngest Son or Where Does Genesis 38 Belong," *Journal of Biblical Literature* 96 (1977) 27–44.

progenitor, as proof in a paternity suit. These objects are not meant simply to reveal her identity; rather their purpose is to establish a link between father and progeny, thereby legitimizing the births of Perez and Zerah. Judah's cord, signet, and staff belong to the same network of signifiers as Joseph's robe or the coat Joseph leaves in the hands of Potiphar's wife. They are the visual markers of a father (or master) and son relationship.

Tamar, like Rebekah, gives birth to twins. While she is in labor, one child puts out a hand to which the midwife attaches a scarlet thread. It is the other child, however, who comes out first. Because the midwife exclaims: "What a breach you made for yourself" (Gen 38:29), the first-born is named Perez, which means "a breach." The second child, the one with the red thread around his wrist, is called Zerah. The birth of Perez and Zerah is emblematic of the Joseph story, for like Zerah, who guides his older brother by widening the birth canal, Joseph as vizier of the Pharaoh directs his older brothers when they come to Egypt to fetch food.

The birth of Perez and Zerah recalls the birth of Esau and Jacob. The two sets of twins form a chiasmus. The "red hairy mantle" which distinguishes Esau, the oldest, becomes the red thread around the youngest's wrist. By wearing Esau's attire, Jacob makes Esau's distinguishing marking—namely, his "red hairy mantle"—his own. Isaac's blessing assures Jacob's superiority over his brother, and the garment becomes the signifier of Jacob's prominence. Similarly, when Jacob gives Joseph a long robe with sleeves, it symbolizes Joseph's superiority; and, when the bloodied robe is returned to Jacob, it signals Joseph's elimination from the line of succession. In Egypt, his brothers may well bow before him, but it is not Joseph's progeny that will assure the might of the people of Israel. That task, as we know, will be assumed by Judah's descendant, for Reuben, Jacob's oldest, had sexual intercourse with Bilhah, his father's concubine (Gen 35:22), thus revealing himself unworthy of his father's trust. It is therefore fitting that in his blessing to his sons, Jacob should distinguish Judah, his chosen heir, by his red garment, thereby bestowing upon him, albeit metaphorically, the symbolic marker of genuine legacy. Judah, Jacob tells us, "washes his garments in wine and his vesture in the blood of grapes" (Gen 49:11). In Genesis, Jacob's line of descent stops with the description of the birth of Perez and Zerah; the fact that it is not Zerah but Perez who is named in the ancestry of David (Matt 1:3) suggests that the sibling rivalries characteristic of the Jacob cycle continued beyond the events recounted in Genesis. However, since the eventual ascendancy of Perez lies outside the context of Genesis, it plays no part in the narrative processes at work in the Jacob cycle. For Michael Fishbane, the power of the Jacob cycle is that "it personalizes the tensions and dialectics which are also crystallized on a national level at later points: the struggle for blessing;

the threat of discontinuity; the conflicts between and within generations; and the wrestling for birth, name and destiny."[7] In the Jacob cycle, garments form the subtext which upholds these concerns. From Jacob to Joseph to Judah to Zerah, the red thread establishes an order of filiation, a metaphorical umbilical cord that relates directly, without the mediation of women, father to son to grandson.

As the Judah and Tamar episode illustrates, in such a system what matters is not who bears the child but the identity of the father. In this male-marked genealogy, women have no say. Their role is strictly biological. The womb as the relevant place of origin is superseded by the progenitor's authority, and ranking of siblings becomes a father's prerogative. It is therefore not surprising that Jacob favors Joseph not because he is the firstborn of his beloved Rachel but because Joseph is "the son of *his* old age" (Gen 37:3).

Following the path of Claude Lévi-Strauss, Judah Goldin reminds us that stories function somewhat like myths for they provide acceptable channels for the expression of discontent:

> The law of God may not be abolished, and besides, for the most part, the society assents to its terms because without these there would be chaos. But the resentments are nonetheless real! How are these to find an outlet? By folktales and folklore. Here no frontal attack is made on the divine law. That is the policy of rebellion. But in stories and fables one turns the order of the world up side down without giving up the establishment that provides protection. This is the revenge of the weak against the strong.[8]

For Judah Goldin, "the revenge of the weak against the strong" refers to the theme of fraternal rivalry and the triumph of the youngest. In order to be counted once again among Jacob's sons, Joseph uses a personal item as a ploy to force recognition. The silver divination cup he has placed in Benjamin's sack of grain (Gen 44:2) serves as an excuse to get his brothers to stand before him so that he can reveal his identity to them. Joseph's stratagem recalls the ploys of Rebekah, Potiphar's wife, and Tamar, who like him use objects as the mediating device for their own personal ends. Sibling rivalry and the ensuing importance of the father and son bond erase the privilege of rank among wives and reduces women's function strictly to their reproductive role. In such a patriarchal system, women are still needed, but they are nonetheless outsiders. When Rebekah, Potiphar's wife, or Tamar uses a piece of attire for their own personal ends, they do not create a gratuitous disturbance

---

[7] Michael Fishbane, "Composition and Structure in the Jacob Cycle (Gen. 25:19–35:22)," *Journal of Jewish Studies* 26 (1975) 38.

[8] Goldin, "The Youngest Son," 44.

in the order of things. Although in a world under divine guidance their actions can be said to actualize the Lord's will, these actions can also be seen as the expression of women's resentment and rebellion. When Rebekah suggests that Jacob take his brother's place, or when Potiphar's wife tries to seduce Joseph, or Tamar calls attention to Judah's progeny, their interference breaks up the exclusive father–son dialogue and forces recognition of their presence. It is therefore not surprising that, in the cycle of Jacob, the women use pieces of attire—which are the symbolic markers of the father–son relationship—to reinscribe themselves in the patriarchal system. Their intervention in the sequence of events ruptures the continuum of the narrative and reveals the patterns interwoven in the textual fabric. In the latter part of Genesis, garments have his and her story to tell: as used by men, garments form a communicative channel from which women are excluded; but when used by women, garments function as communicative devices between the sexes. For the men, garments are symbolic markers of filial love and recognition, whereas for the women they serve as a means of self-inscription in a system that neglects them. In her article "On Me Be the Curse, My Son!" Christine Garside Allen argues that, in securing for Jacob Isaac's blessing meant for Esau, Rebekah was only carrying out God's wishes. For Allen, it is not Isaac but Rebekah who through her selfless obedience shows herself to be a model of sanctity. "It is tempting," she writes, "to bring Rebekah into relief by maintaining that Isaac was not a saint. In this way Rebekah would be the necessary link between Abraham and Jacob."[9] Christine Garside Allen's analysis clearly shows that, even if seen as a consecrated deed and interpreted from a psychological viewpoint, Rebekah's deceitful action ultimately disturbs the exclusively male genealogical lineage.

For Isaac, as for Jacob and Judah, garments have a fixed meaning: Esau's tunic and Joseph's robe represent specific individuals. Isaac mistakes the garment for the wearer and thus gives his blessing to Jacob instead of Esau. As for Judah, he is unable to recognize his daughter-in-law behind the prostitute's veil. Whereas for the men garments have a determined, precise meaning, that is to say, a truth value, for the women clothes are nothing but signifiers open to a variety of meanings; they are items whose function and referential meaning can easily be changed. When Tamar exchanges her widow's dress for the prostitute's veil, she simultaneously calls attention to two social functions of garments: first, their use as symbols in the sexual code; and, second, their use as masks and disguises. When Potiphar's wife points to Joseph's coat at her side as

---

[9] Christine Garside Allen, "On Me Be the Curse, My Son!" *Encounter with the Text: Form and History in the Hebrew Bible* (ed. Martin J. Buss; Philadelphia: Fortress, 1979) 168–69.

the proof of Joseph's attempt to seduce her, her story is believable because she provides a sexual significance to an item which, in the social context, can have a sexual referential meaning. She also uses Joseph's coat to hide her own sexual desire. Because for women, garments do not necessarily refer to a specific individual or convey solely one message, they are the place of juncture for a multiplicity of meanings, the locus for the expression of divergent desires. For Tamar, as for Potiphar's wife or Rebekah, garments are the means by which they impart their desire to play a relevant role in the patriarchal hierarchy. By pluralizing the meaning of a piece of attire, Rebekah, Potiphar's wife, and Tamar explode and thereby subvert the closure of the patriarchal representational system and symbolic code. Thus, in the latter part of Genesis, the function of garments, as understood by the women of the cycle of Jacob, can serve as the very metaphor for textuality and the deconstructive nature of modern reading practices which Barbara Johnson describes as "a careful teasing out of warring forces of signification within the text."[10] The patterns woven in the biblical narrative take their shape from the filling as well as the warp; the two strands may have different functions, but they are equally necessary to the making of the textual fabric.

Because it can be construed as a representation of different critical approaches, the episode between Joseph and Potiphar's wife (Genesis 39) provided me with a point of entry into the text. Joseph rejects the advances of his master's wife and runs out of the house leaving his coat behind. Potiphar's wife tells her husband that Joseph tried to seduce her; Potiphar believes her and Joseph is incarcerated. Potiphar accepts his wife's explanation because her story does seem plausible, after all. And besides, since for the men in the Jacob cycle garments are a sign of trust and have a symbolic power that lends them even more verity, in the eyes of Potiphar Joseph's "abandoned" coat gives added credence to his wife's words. However, in accepting his wife's explanation as stated, Potiphar ignores the possibility of personal motivation. He is blind not only to his wife's self-serving reasons, but equally blind to what may be his own reasons for wanting to believe her. Potiphar's attitude is an example of a critical perspective that leaves unquestioned both the subjective needs of the storyteller and the conscious or unconscious investment of the interpreter. Yet for each of the characters in this episode, the coat has a special meaning. For Joseph and the biblical narrator, the coat stands as the proof of Joseph's innocence; for Potiphar's wife, it is the reminder of her frustrated desire; for her husband, the evidence of Joseph's guilt. Joseph's coat is the place of juncture for diverging desires. The textual fabric of a narrative is similarly the locus and the product of

[10] Barbara Johnson, "The Critical Difference," *Diacritics* 8 (Summer 1978) 3.

the interaction of the narrator's and the reader's subjectivities. Not unlike the story told by Potiphar's wife, my version of the stories in the Jacob cycle may be warped, skewed by my feminist and critical concerns. But, on the other hand, the anonymous biblical narrator wages for Joseph's innocence. In siding with Joseph, the narrator embraces the ideological structure which Joseph serves, namely, the male desire for an exclusive bond between men. On the question of family lineage or on the subject of human relationships, the position of the biblical narrator is no more "neutral" than that of the feminist reader.

7

THE LITERARY CHARACTERIZATION OF MOTHERS
AND SEXUAL POLITICS IN THE HEBREW BIBLE

Esther Fuchs

The impact of the Hebrew Bible on the present state of sexual politics has been universally recognized by feminist critics.[1] Nevertheless, few of them went beyond the aetiological myth of Genesis 2–3 to demonstrate the patriarchal conception of the Bible.[2] The story of woman's creation from man and his subsequent victimization by her is unquestionably one of the most influential stories in Western literary tradition, but it is not the only biblical story that addresses the power-structured relations between men and women. It is indeed astonishing that the recent spate of feminist literary critiques has not yet produced a single consistent analysis of the literary strategies deployed by the biblical narrative to promote its patriarchal ideology.[3] As a part of a forthcoming comprehensive study of the literary strategies of biblical patriarchalism, whose major goal is to analyze the ideological determinants of female characters in the Hebrew Bible, the present study focuses on the biblical characterization of the mother figure.

Although certain female biblical characters create the impression that "the story belongs" to them and to "chance" as Phyllis Trible asserts, they are for the most part a product of biblical patriarchal legislation.[4]

---

[1] "Sexual politics" refers to the power-structured relations between men and women and more specifically to the economic, social, and ideological arrangements whereby males have traditionally controlled females. This definition is based on Kate Millet, *Sexual Politics* (New York: Ballantine, 1969) 31–81. "Biblical sexual politics" refers to the ways in which the Bible promotes the idea of woman's subordination to man.

[2] "Patriarchy" and all its derivative forms refer here to the ideological and social system based on the subordination of women and younger males to adult males.

[3] Mary Daly's *Beyond God the Father* (Boston: Beacon, 1973) employs a philosophical method in exposing and analyzing the patriarchal underpinnings of Judeo-Christian tradition. Judith Ochshorn's *The Female Experience and the Nature of the Divine* (Bloomington: Indiana University Press, 1981) uses mostly historical and theological perspectives.

[4] Phyllis Trible, *God and the Rhetoric of Sexuality* (Philadelphia: Fortress, 1978) 178. Trible attempts to highlight suppressed evidence for what appears to be woman's point of view in the Hebrew Bible, ignoring the patriarchal determinants of this point of view. For

The "legislative" aspect of female characterization is not unique to the biblical narrative. As feminist critics have demonstrated, patriarchal didacticism informs most classical literary works revolving around woman, including the supposedly descriptive ones. Since until very recently the literary scene was dominated by male authors, it is not surprising that the female characters reveal more about the wishful thinking, fears, aspirations, and prejudices of their male creators than about women's authentic lives. Concluding a story about a clandestine love affair with the heroine's suicide (i.e., *Anna Karenina, Madame Bovary*), for example, reflects the author's attitude to adultery as much as, if not more than, it reflects historical reality.[5] As Wayne Booth has demonstrated, an "objective" or "neutral" reflection of reality in literature is nothing more than an artistic illusion.[6] The author's point of view determines the ideological framework of the story even when it seems to be altogether absent from it.

The fact is that the ideological aspect prevails in all literary characterization. The ascription of motivation, thought, action, and word to a certain character constitutes an indirect means of authorial judgment which exists even in what appears to be the most neutral and objective tale. The "pragmatic" level of the literary narrative pertaining to the author–reader relationship is inherent in the very nature of the literary composition;[7] it is especially obtrusive in the biblical narrative, which is patently didactic.[8] Yet while the monotheistic didacticism of the biblical

---

example, she considers the book of Ruth as a story that extols woman's initiative and independence in a man's world (p. 166). She ignores the fact that Ruth does not act independently but complies strictly with the patriarchal ethos which enjoins woman to remain eternally faithful to her husband and his family. Ruth renounces her own culture and heritage, in order to follow her mother-in-law, Naomi, the mother of her husband, not just any woman. Ruth is extolled for the patronymic and patrilineal continuity of her dead husband's family. She sacrifices her own freedom and identity in order to perpetuate the identity of her late husband and father-in-law.

[5] It is impossible to offer an exhaustive list of feminist works dealing with literary images of women as expressions of a male world view. Some of the best examples include Kate Millet's *Sexual Politics*, 3–30; Simone de Beauvoir's *The Second Sex*, (trans. and ed. H. M. Parshley; New York: Vintage, 1952) 224–300. On myths and narratives reflecting male fears see H. R. Hays, *The Dangerous Sex—The Myth of Feminine Evil* (New York: Putnam and Sons, 1964); on female literary stereotypes see Mary Ellman, *Thinking About Women* (New York: Harcourt Brace and World, 1968).

[6] Wayne C. Booth, *The Rhetoric of Fiction* (Chicago: University of Chicago Press, 1961).

[7] The term "pragmatic" is borrowed from Boris Uspensky, *A Poetics of Composition* (Berkeley and Los Angeles: University of California Press, 1973).

[8] This is not the place to go into the thorny issue of biblical didactic strategies and techniques of authorial judgment. Despite pervasive scholarly disagreement, some progress has been made in this area. See for example Meir Sternberg and Menakhem Perry, "*Hamelek be'mabat ironi*" [The King through Ironic Eyes], *Hasifrut* 1:2 (Summer 1968) 263–92; Boaz Arpali, "*Zehirut; sipur miqrai*" [Attention; a Biblical Story], *Hasifrut* 2:3 (August

narrative has been largely recognized, its patriarchal ideology has been practically ignored. Thus, for example, it has been widely established that the motif of the miraculous conception of a barren woman in the Bible implies that Yahweh is the sole proprietor and master of human life, which fits well the biblical monotheistic framework. As we shall see, there is also at work a patriarchal ideology, which is closely related to the hierarchical conception of monotheism.[9]

In a thoroughly didactic and economical book like the Bible, it is practically impossible to find pure descriptions. The female characters depicted in the biblical tale are ideologically contrived as much as their male counterparts, and no more than the latter they constitute to a large degree role models. But whereas the male role models are mostly judged in terms of their relations with Yahweh, the female role models are mostly evaluated in terms of their relations with men.

In what follows we shall examine the patriarchal determinants of the biblical characterization of the mother figure. This examination will be based on a comparative study of the annunciation type-scenes and a comparative study of father and mother figures and the power-structured relations between them.

The biblical annunciation type-scene consists of three major thematic components: the initial barrenness of the wife, a divine promise of future conception, and the birth of a son.[10] While these components function largely as constants, the actual scenes vary in narrative span and complexity. As Robert Alter points out, the deflections from the standard structure are not coincidental; they function often as foreshadowing techniques alluding to future events in the life of the future son.[11] For our purpose, the most significant variations pertain to the role of the potential mother in the annunciation type-scene; these variations, as we shall see next, constitute a consistently increasing emphasis on the potential mother as the true heroine of the annunciation type-scene.

The first biblical annunciation type-scene is preceded by Yahweh's direct address to the potential father, Abraham, regarding the future conception of his barren wife, Sarai, "And God said to Abraham, 'As for Sarai your wife you shall not call her name Sarai, but Sarah shall be her

---

1970) 580–97; Meir Sternberg, "*Mivneh hahazara basipur hamiqrai*" [The Structure of Repetition in the Biblical Story], *Hasifrut* 25 (October 1977) 110–50; Yair Hoffman "*Bein Convensia leestrategia*" [Between Convention and Strategy], *Hasifrut* 28 (April 1979) 88–99.

[9] For the relationship of patriarchalism to hierarchical monotheism see Rosemary R. Ruether, *New Woman New Earth* (New York: Seabury, 1975) 1–35. See also Ochshorn, *The Female Experience*, 181–238.

[10] Robert Alter, *The Art of Biblical Narrative* (New York: Basic Books, 1981). For an explanation of the biblical type-scene in general, see pp. 47–52.

[11] Robert Alter, "How Convention Helps Us Read: The Case of the Bible's Annunciation Type-Scene" *Prooftexts* 3/2 (May 1983) 115–30.

name. I will bless her, and moreover I will give you a son by her; I will bless her, and she shall be the mother of nations; kings of peoples shall come from her'" (Gen 17:15–16).[12] Although Sarai's status and thereby her fate are discussed in this dialogue, she is referred to in the third person.

Yahweh blesses Sarai in her absence and changes her name through her husband. The act of naming signifies a recognition of identity, an endowment of new essence and being, and it also implies that the namer has authority over the named. Yahweh changes Abram's name to Abraham (17:5) in his direct dialogue with him, yet the names of his wife and his son, which are also determined by Yahweh, are to be given to Abraham, who represents God's authority as husband and father. More importantly, the blessing of Sarai and the change in her name are preceded by a restatement of Yahweh's covenant with Abraham. The transformation of the barren Sarai into a fertile Sarah is a logical and necessary procedure required by Yahweh's commitment to Abraham: "And I will make my covenant between me and you, and will multiply you exceedingly. . . . Behold the covenant is with you, and you shall be the father of a multitude of nations" (Gen 17:2, 4). Furthermore, the text emphasized that it is Abraham (and not Sarah) who is the true recipient of the promised son: "and I shall also give you a son from her." Verse 19 repeats this emphasis: ". . . and also Sarah your wife is bearing *you* a son. . . ." The son is to be born *to* and *for* (*lĕ*) Abraham *by* Sarah. Sarah's status as primarily the *means* of reproduction, the instrument through which God will keep his promise to Abraham, cannot be gainsaid.

In the annunciation type-scene itself Abraham continues to occupy center stage. The scene opens with an introductory verse that leaves no doubt about the actual addressee of Yahweh: "And the Lord appeared to him by the oaks of Mamre, as he sat in the tent door in the heat of the day" (18:1). When the three messengers arrive at the tent, Abraham, the generous and hospitable host, invites the guests to rest and refresh themselves, while instructing Sarah, who is inside the tent, to prepare cakes for the men. Sarah's function in this context is no different from that of Abraham's servant, who is enjoined to prepare a calf for the meal. Unlike Abraham, who is implicitly praised for his generosity and eagerness to please his guests, Sarah, who is not privy to what is happening outside the tent, receives no credit for her work, since she functions as her husband's adjunct. Throughout the meal Sarah shows no interest in the guests. The text repeats the fact that Sarah remains inside the tent in Abraham's response to the messengers' query concerning her whereabouts (18:9). This

---

[12] This and all the following quotations are based on the *Revised Standard Version* with occasional revisions, unless otherwise stated.

repetition is not coincidental; it emphasizes Sarah's absence from this fateful scene and, in contrast, Abraham's central role in it. Instead of becoming actively involved in the conversation Sarah eavesdrops on her husband and guests "at the tent door behind him" [Abraham] (v 10). Once again, although Sarah is the subject of Yahweh's address, she is referred to in the third person while her husband functions as the actual addressee: "Yahweh said, 'I shall surely return to you when the season comes round and Sarah your wife shall have a son'" (v 10).[13] Even when Sarah is reprimanded for laughing to herself in disbelief, she is addressed through her husband. Only when she denies having laughed, does Yahweh speak directly to her, "saying, 'No, but you did laugh'" (v 15). Yahweh's only direct reference to Sarah takes the form of an implicit accusation.

The juxtaposition of the husband and the wife in this scene enhances the attributes of the former and the drawbacks of the latter. Abraham's activity outside the tent is contrasted with Sarah's passivity. Seventeen verbs predicate Abraham's dedication to his guests. The verbs "run" and "hasten" are repeated twice. Sarah, on the other hand, is the subject of four verbs, none of which demonstrates a high level of exertion: to hear, laugh, deny, and fear. Although there is reason to believe that Sarah obeyed her husband's instructions and, like a good housewife, baked cakes for the guests, the text does not mention this fact explicitly. Sarah emerges from the scene as confined, passive, cowardly, deceptive, and above all untrusting of Yahweh's omnipotence.[14] Sarah's participation in the annunciation type-scene amounts to a troublesome interference. She is not only inferior to Abraham in the literary sense, as a secondary character, but in a moral and spiritual sense as well. If the text is trying to establish a correlation between Yahweh's benevolence and the uprightness of his subjects, it is clear that the manifestation of this benevolence, namely, the annunciation type-scene, is related causally to the man's demeanor and concessively to the woman's. The implication is that Yahweh violates nature's rules and gives the barren woman a child because of her husband's magnanimity and despite her pettiness. But the fulfillment of the divine promise does not follow the annunciation in the narrative sequence; instead, it is postponed until chap. 21, which opens with a characteristic formula: "And the Lord remembered Sarah" (Gen 21:1). The interpolated narrative material refers to Abraham's intercession in behalf of the citizens of Sodom and Gomorrah, the destruction of the iniquitous cities by Yahweh (chap. 19) and the episode in Gerar in which

---

[13] "$K\bar{a}$'$\bar{e}t$ $hayy\hat{a}$," is translated by RSV "in the spring." Here I use the Jewish Publication Society version (Philadelphia, 1955).

[14] Although Abraham too laughs at the prospect of having a child in his old age (Gen 17:17), Yahweh does not rebuke him for his faithlessness but instead reassures him that the promise will be realized.

Abraham presents his wife as his sister (chap. 20). Sarah is absent from chap. 19, which dramatizes Abraham's compassion and altruism. In chap. 20, she appears as a passive object of sexual possession, taken by Abimelech, King of Gerar, and narrowly saved from committing adultery by the direct intervention of Yahweh.

Although Sarah is given full credit for giving birth to Isaac, in chap. 21, the text continues to stress that she is mostly instrumental and that the miracle is performed for Abraham. Verse 2 does not simply state the fact that Sarah bore a son but that "she bore Abraham a son." Verse 3 repeats this idea twice: "Abraham called the name of his son who was born to him, whom Sarah bore him, Isaac." Abraham proceeds to establish his paternal authority over his newborn son, by naming and circumcising him (21:4), while Sarah comments again on the risibility of her belated conception (21:6).

As we noted, the first annunciation type-scene starts with Yahweh's address to Abraham, without being previously solicited by either Abraham or Sarah. In the second annunciation type-scene, Isaac initiates the first move; he pleads with Yahweh in behalf of his barren wife and Yahweh grants his prayer (Gen 25:21). Once again, the wife's conception is attributed to the good relationship of her husband with Yahweh; it is not contingent upon the qualities or actions of the wife. Nevertheless, it is Yahweh's response to Rebekah that the text reports and not his response to Isaac. In response to Rebekah's complaint about her painful pregnancy, Yahweh explains that she is bearing twins and that the younger of the two will prevail over the older. Whereas in the first annunciation type-scene Yahweh discusses the future son with the father, here he shares his prescience with the mother. Another indication of Rebekah's greater involvement in the future of her children occurs in their naming. Whereas in the case of Isaac Yahweh endows Abraham with the exclusive right to name his son, here the children are named by both parents: "The first came forth red, all his body like a hairy mantle; so *they* called his name Esau. Afterward, his brother came forth . . . so his name was called Jacob" (Gen 25:25–26).[15] Unlike Sarah, Rebekah appears at center stage, alongside Isaac. She receives greater recognition from Yahweh as potential mother, and there is not so much as an allusion to a moral discrepancy between the man and his wife, at this point.

The third annunciation type-scene is preceded by a description of the plight and despair of the barren wife. The text presents Rachel as a jealous co-wife, exasperated by the fertility of her rival, Leah. In her despair, Rachel turns to Jacob with an impetuous and largely childish demand: "Give me children, or I shall die" (Gen 30:1). The reader is

[15] The Hebrew in verse 26 reads "and he called his name Jacob," but it does not specify a subject; it is therefore acceptable to render it in the passive form.

expected to sympathize with Jacob's angry response: "Am I in the place of God who has withheld from you the fruit of the womb?" (30:2). Indeed, the previous type-scenes bear Jacob's statement out, for was it not Yahweh who gave Sarah and Rebekah children? Robert Alter suggests a causal connection between Rachel's attitude and the fact that none of her sons became progenitors of the royal seed; he also suggests that Rachel's death following Benjamin's birth may be related to her failure to perceive Yahweh's exclusive control of birth. Yet Rachel's request is not altogether unjustifiable considering the concern that Isaac, for example, shows for his wife in the preceding type-scene. Her petulant demand could be interpreted by a more indulgent husband as, "Why don't you pray for me? Do something, I'm desperate." Jacob's response, however, all but ignores the perlocutionary aspect of Rachel's blatant words. Not only does he fail to share her plight, he chastises her angrily and self-righteously. Jacob's reaction implies that his wife's barrenness is outside his sphere of control; he disclaims all responsibility for his wife's condition. The ensuing list of the sons born to Jacob by other concubines and by Leah intimates that Jacob may not be concerned because his progeny was ensured by other means. Finally, the conventional formula announcing divine intervention appears: "Then God remembered Rachel, and God hearkened to her and opened her womb" (30:22). The formula differs from both previous formulas of divine intervention. The first formula presents Yahweh's intervention as a fulfillment of a promise: "The Lord visited Sarah as he had said, and the Lord did to Sarah as he had promised" (21:1). The second formula presents divine intervention as a direct response to the husband's plea: ". . . the Lord granted his prayer" (25:21). The third formula, however, stresses the fact that Yahweh intervenes in response to Rachel's plight, by repeating that He "remembered her" (*wayyizkōr*) "and hearkened to her" (*wayyišma‘*) (30:22). In addition, Rachel, like Leah, reserves the right of naming her sons. Jacob accepts the names given to his sons by his wives with the exception of Benjamin.[16]

Although Jacob does not perform a central role in this type-scene, he emerges from it victorious. His treatment of his wife may not be exemplary, but his awe of Yahweh is, and in biblical terms, this is the ultimate benchmark of the evaluation of a male character.

The fourth annunciation type-scene, on the other hand, presents the potential father, Manoah, as something of a schlemiel, whereas his unnamed wife emerges as the clear protagonist of the scene. Manoah is absent when the angel of the Lord appears to his wife and informs her that she is to conceive a son who will be a Nazirite and a national

---

[16] Jacob changes the name Rachel gives to her second son from *ben-'ônî* ("the son of my sorrow"), to *binyāmîn* ("the son of my right hand") (Gen 35:18).

redeemer (Judg 13:3–5). Not only is the woman apprised of the future of her son, but she is given a set of instructions to follow during her pregnancy, implying a close interdependence between the mother's actions and the future son's life. When Manoah hears the news, he entreats the Lord to send his messenger once again. When the angel reappears, it is once again the woman who sees him first, while sitting alone in the field. The open field points up metonymically the woman's independence, just as the tent underscored Sarah's confinement. Similarly, the words "and Manoah arose and went after his wife" (v 11) signify the husband's dependence on his wife. This constitutes a reverse analogy to the posture of Sarah inside the tent behind Abraham (Gen 18:10).

In response to Manoah's repetitious questions, the angel repeats his instructions to the woman, adding nothing at all to what he had previously said to Manoah's wife and to what she had already reported to her husband. Whereas the woman perceives immediately that the messenger is "a man of God" and compares his appearance to the "countenance of an angel of God, very terrible" (Judg 13:6), Manoah treats the divine messenger as a human being, inviting him for a meal. When the angel declines Manoah's invitation, hinting at his divine identity by suggesting that Manoah should use the meal as a burnt offering for the Lord, Manoah misses the hint and proceeds to inquire about the stranger's name, so that "when your words come true, we may honor you" (v 17). This request contrasts with the woman's conscientious and respectful silence (Judg 13:6). Even when the stranger answers enigmatically, pointing out that his name is "wondrous" (or "mysterious"), Manoah remains unaware of the stranger's true identity. Only when he witnesses the miraculous ascent to heaven in the flame of the burnt offering, "*Then* Manoah knew that he was the angel of the Lord" (v 21). The emphasis on the temporal adverb at the beginning of the sentence adds an additional dash of irony to the satirical presentation of the obtuse husband. But now Manoah panics: "We shall surely die, for we have seen God" (v 22). Once again, Manoah's wife demonstrates her superior intelligence by pointing out the futility of showing miracles to people who had been singled out for death. The text vindicates her point of view by following this interchange with the final component of the annunciation type-scene, the fulfillment of the divine promise: "And the woman bore a son and called his name Samson" (v 24). The woman does not bear a son "to" her husband; neither does she consult her husband about their son's name.

The thematic and structural parallels between Judges 13 and Genesis 18 highlight the radical shift in the characterization and respective status of the potential mother and father figures. Whereas the hospitality of Abraham is graciously accepted by the three messengers, Manoah's hospitality is rejected. The first scene uses Abraham's hospitality to enhance his uprightness, the latter exposes Manoah's hospitality as maladroitness. In the first scene, Yahweh addresses Sarah indirectly and peripherally; in the fourth scene God turns to the woman first and only repeats for her husband things already known to her. Sarah emerges from the first scene as a skeptical and parochial housewife, vastly overshadowed by Abraham's magnanimity. Manoah's wife, on the other hand, is perspicacious, sensitive, and devout, outshining her inept husband. Sarah's unnecessary interference in the course of the first annunciation type-scene parallels to a great extent the dispensable contributions of Manoah.

In the next scene, the potential father is pushed even further away from the focus of the story. Hannah, like Rachel, suffers not only from her barrenness but also from the provocations of Peninnah, her fertile rival. But, unlike Rachel, Hannah does not turn to her husband, Elkanah, for help. She decides to address her plea directly to Yahweh. She does not even call on Eli, the priest, who is visibly stationed by the doorposts of the temple; instead she pours out her bitter heart in prayer and directly enlists God's help, by offering to dedicate her future son to his service. This is the first time that the barren woman is shown to turn directly to Yahweh; Rebekah, it will be remembered, turns to Yahweh to complain of her difficult pregnancy, not to entreat him for children. This is also the first time that the type-scene reports in direct speech the barren woman's prayer for children.

Hannah circumvents the authority of both Elkanah and Eli by making a vow to Yahweh on her own initiative. The text implies support for her initiative by pointing out that Elkanah fails to understand his wife's misery (1 Sam 1:8) and by satirizing Eli as an obtuse old man who misinterprets Hannah's chagrin for drunkenness. Sure of his perception, he rebukes the embittered woman with harsh words: "How long will you be drunken? Put away your wine from you" (1:14). But confronted with Hannah's eloquent response, Eli retracts his rash accusation and bids the woman to go in peace, adding: "and the God of Israel grant your petition which you made to him" (1:17). It is not clear whether Eli is promising Yahweh's help or merely expressing his wishful blessings. Either way, Eli remains unaware of Hannah's specific request, which does not add much to his already suspect stature as divine oracle and representative of Yahweh.

Unlike the preceding divine messengers, Eli fails to anticipate the miraculous conception. Whereas the previous messengers anticipate and initiate the annunciation, Eli *reacts* to Hannah's initiative. Furthermore, Eli fails to understand Hannah's plight and, although he reacts favorably to her plea, the text implies that he remains unaware of its specific nature.

Neither does Elkanah, the potential father, understand Hannah's anguish. "And Elkanah, her husband, said to her, 'Hannah, why do you weep? And why do you not eat? Any why is your heart sad? Am I not more to you than ten sons?'" (1 Sam 1:8). Elkanah's repeated questions indicate his concern for his wife, but at the same time they imply help-lessness and a basic lack of understanding for the childless woman. Elkanah's speech functions as ironic self-betrayal; it dramatizes the husband's exaggerated sense of self-importance and his inability to real-ize that his love cannot compensate for his wife's barrenness. Elkanah's lack of insight into what the bible presents as woman's greatest tragedy places him in a marginal role within the framework of this drama. Unlike the previous husbands, who came into direct contact with divine emissaries (or, in Jacob's case, spoke on behalf of Yahweh), Elkanah is absent from the scene dramatizing the divine element.

In his capacity as Yahweh's representative, Eli promises Hannah God's help. Fulfilling his role as husband, Elkanah has intercourse with his wife, but neither of these male characters is shown to have any awareness of the special significance of his actions. Both Eli and Elkanah are excluded from the privileged point of view of Hannah, the omni-scient narrator, and the implied reader. Juxtaposed with these male foils, Hannah emerges as the incontestable heroine of the scene. Whereas in the case of Sarah the text emphasizes that she bore a son "to Abraham," here the text presents the husband as an auxiliary character: "And Elkanah knew Hannah his wife, and the Lord remembered her, and in due time Hannah conceived and bore a son, and she called his name Samuel, for she said, 'I have asked him of the Lord'" (1 Sam 1:19–20).

If Elkanah may be defined as "Card," the potential father in the final annunciation type-scene functions barely as "ficelle."[17] Gehazi, Elisha's servant, describes him as an old man (2 Kgs 4:14). The text dramatizes him as uninsightful and passive. His contribution to the annunciation scene proper is all but marginal. Before the son's birth, the potential father is referred to only in the third person. He is practically excluded from the interaction between the man of God, Elisha, and his wife, who is called "the great woman of Shunem."[18] The Shunammite is the one who goes out of her way to "seize" Elisha, offering him meals whenever he passes through town.[19] Discontent with her sporadic hospi-tality, she convinces her husband to dedicate a room in their house for Elisha. The text records the woman's suggestion in great detail and omits the husband's reply, thereby underscoring the woman's initiative and, in contrast, the husband's passivity and possibly indifference.

This annunciation type-scene is the first to present the female pro-tagonist as character before focusing on her as a maternal role model.

---

[17] "Card" refers to a secondary character; "ficelle" to a peripheral one (W. J. Harvey, *Character and the Novel* [Ithaca, NY: Cornell University Press, 1965]).

[18] Here I prefer the King James and the JPS version to the RSV, which renders the Hebrew word gĕdôlâ as "wealthy."

[19] The Hebrew verb wattaḥăzeq is much more expressive than the more figurative trans-lation "urged" (RSV) or "constrained" (KJV and JPS).

The actions and speeches of the preceding female characters were mostly motivated by the desire for children or by the prospect of giving birth. These characters were described only in conjunction with the binary theme of barrenness–fertility or with the fate and identity of their prospective sons. In the case of the great woman of Shunem, her character and her relationship with Elisha seem to deserve attention independently of the theme of childlessness. The text insists that the Shunammite's hospitality and generosity stem from her benevolence, not from an ulterior motive. When urged by Elisha to express her needs, in return for her favors, the Shunammite demurs: "I dwell among my own people" is her proud answer (2 Kgs 4:13). Only when Gehazi, Elisha's servant, informs him that the woman "has no son, and her husband is old" (v 14) does the reader realize that the Shunammite is childless. This is the first time that the annunciation type-scene does not attribute childlessness exclusively to woman. The text does not define the woman as "barren" ('ăqārâ) or closed-wombed; on the contrary, by specifying that her husband is old, the text suggests that the man's age may explain the absence of children this time. When Elisha informs her that "at this season, when the time comes round, you shall embrace a son" (2 Kgs 4:16), she is incredulous: "No, my lord, Oh man of God; do not lie to your maidservant" (v 16). By introducing the woman's qualities before the actual annunciation, the narrative establishes a relationship of cause and effect between the episodes. This type-scene is the first to present Yahweh's intervention as *reward for woman's upright conduct*. Hannah conceives, thanks to her ardent prayer to Yahweh; the Shunammite conceives, thanks to her selflessness, benevolence, humility, and loyalty to Yahweh's emissary.

The first type-scene establishes a causal link between the husband's uprightness and the wife's miraculous conception. The text makes it clear that the postmenopausal and barren Sarah conceives not because of her own conduct but thanks to Yahweh's interest in Abraham. The hospitality, generosity, and humility initially ascribed to the potential father are now ascribed to the potential mother. On the other hand, the reticence, passivity, and indifference displayed by the potential mother toward the divine messengers in the first type-scene are transposed to the potential father in the last. It is significant that the text does not stress that the Shunammite bore a son "to" or even *by* her husband; omitting the husband from the final phase of the scene, it states: "But the woman conceived and bore a son about that time the following spring, as Elisha said to her" (v 17).

The passivity of the Shunammite's husband is further dramatized in his reaction to his son's disease and subsequent death. When the boy complains of a severe headache, his father orders a servant to "carry him to his mother" (v 19). When the Shunammite hurries to see Elisha, her

husband, unaware of the disaster, argues: "Why will you go to him
today? It is neither new moon nor Sabbath" (v 23). The husband's protes-
tations expose his limited understanding of the events. His criticism of
his wife backfires. The husband's unanswered questions function here as
irony of self-betrayal. As in Elkanah's case, these questions are potential
obstructions rather than accelerating factors in the plot progression
toward the happy denouement. Whereas Hannah leaves Elkanah's questions unanswered, the Shunammite responds to her old man's irrelevant
arguments with a short "šālôm" ("It shall be well" [v 23]).

Yet the husband is not the only character ridiculed by the narrative.
I tend to agree with Robert Alter that the narrator of 2 Kings is rather
ambivalent toward the figure of Elisha in general.[20] In our particular
scene, Elisha is not aware that his benefactress is childless and acts in her
behalf only after Gehazi apprises him of the situation. Furthermore,
when the Shunammite comes to see him concerning her dead son, he is
unaware of the disaster and instructs his servant to greet her and ask her
if it is well with her, her husband, and her son (v 26). Realizing that the
woman is in great distress he admits that the "Lord has hidden it from
me, and has not told me" (v 27). Elisha remains in the dark until the
Shunammite speaks; but instead of hurrying to the dead boy, he dis-
patches his servant Gehazi, instructing him to put his staff on the boy's
face (similar to the husband who sends the sick boy to his mother with a
servant)—a solution that proves later to be ineffective. Only when the
woman insists on his personal involvement does Elisha consent to follow
her (v 30). The detailed description of Elisha's technical attempts to
revive the dead son presents the process of resuscitation as a medical
rather than miraculous ordeal. Despite the woman's impeccable conduct
and profound piety, Elisha continues to refer to her as "the Shunammite" and sometimes with the more derisive "that Shunammite" (haššû-
nammît hallāz [v 25]), as if he never condescended to learn her name.
But clearly Elisha's attitude is not representative of the narrator's point
of view.

The growing recognition of the potential mother figure suggests an
ever increasing emphasis within the biblical framework on the institution
of motherhood. As Adrienne Rich points out, the social and legal *institution* of motherhood is distinctly different from the personal and psychological aspect of motherhood; the latter refers to "the *potential relationship* of
any woman to her powers of reproduction and to children," whereas the

---

[20] Alter suggests that Elisha's lying on the boy and breathing life into his dead body is a
parodic allusion to the creation scene in which Yahweh breathes life into the nostrils of
the first man. He also points out the satiric judgment implied in Elisha's ursine massacre
of the boys who had taunted him for his baldness (2 Kgs 2:23–25). See Alter, "How Convention Helps Us Read," 126.

former refers to the mechanism aimed at "ensuring that that potential—and all women—shall remain under male control."[21] The institution of motherhood is a powerful patriarchal mechanism. Male control of female reproductive powers in conjunction with patrilocal and monogamous marriage (for the wife), secures the wife as her husband's exclusive property and ensures the continuity of his name and family possessions through patrinomial customs and patrilineal inheritance patterns. The institution of motherhood as defined by the patriarchal system guarantees that both the wife and her children will increase his property during his lifetime and perpetuate his achievements and memory after his death.

The annunciation type-scenes surveyed in this study clearly define motherhood as patriarchal institution, *not* as personal tendency of woman. All the mother figures in these scenes are married wives. There is no instance in the biblical narrative in which an unmarried barren woman is visited by God or divine emissary and miraculously released from her barrenness. This would be unthinkable, since the child born out of wedlock would not be able to carry on his father's lineage and would be ostracized from the community as a "*mamzēr*" (Deut 23:3), while his mother would at best be branded as zônâ ("whore"). Yahweh, in the biblical narrative, restricts his interest in barren women to married women and to situations that leave no doubt about the identity of the potential father. What seems to be a sentimental narrative about the happy transition from emptiness to fullness and from failure to victory is a carefully constructed story intended among other things to promote the institution of motherhood. All the narrative details are designed and orchestrated in accordance with this ideological perspective, from the selection of thematic materials to the organization of motifs, dialogue, plot structure, and characterization. The growing emphasis on the figure of the potential mother may be misinterpreted as a growing recognition of the importance of woman's reproductive powers. The fact is that the annunciation type-scene, in its many variations, drives home the opposite message: that woman has no control at all over her reproductive potential. Yahweh, who is often andromorphized in the biblical narrative, has control. Furthermore, all the divine messengers, dispatched to proclaim the imminent miraculous conception, are male figures. The literary constellation of male characters surrounding and determining the fate of the potential mother dramatizes the idea that woman's reproductive potential should be and can be controlled only by men. It is true that the presence of the potential husband progressively decreases in the annunciation type-scene, but his presence is nevertheless essential.

Tamar, Judah's daughter-in-law, would have been burned at the stake and condemned as a harlot had she tried to procure children outside of her

[21] *Of Woman Born* (New York: Norton, 1976) xv (italics are original).

deceased husband's family (Gen 38:24). The only thing that saves her life and turns her into a biblical heroine is the fact that the man she sleeps with, Judah, is directly related to Er, her deceased husband, who left her with no children. Ruth, too, is extolled as a heroine, thanks to her faithfulness to her deceased husband's patrilineage. What turns her into a biblical heroine is not the fact that she prefers to follow Naomi to the land of Judah rather than to stay in Moab, but the fact that Naomi is her mother-in-law, the mother of Mahlon, her deceased husband who left her childless. She is not merely extolled for her ability to survive physically in adverse circumstances or for her initiative and energy in general, as some would have it, but for her success in finding and marrying a direct relative of Elimelech, her father-in-law, and giving birth to children who would carry on the patrilineage of her deceased husband.[22]

Tamar and Ruth achieve the high status of biblical heroines, thanks to their voluntary and active support of the patriarchal institution of the levirate, which insures the patrilineage of a deceased husband.[23] But the biblical narrative is careful *not* to establish too close a link between the interests of patriarchy and woman's sacrifice. On the contrary, the heroine's motivation is normally shown to be self-seeking. Both Ruth and Tamar are shown to fight for their *own* benefit and security; this may of course be an authentic reflection of the patriarchal society that encouraged women to become lawful mothers by elevating the mother's social status.[24] At the same time, it constitutes a powerful ideological strategy. By projecting onto woman what man desires most, the biblical narrative creates a powerful role model for women. The image of the childless woman (barren wife or widow) who evolves from vulnerability and emptiness to security and pride by giving birth to sons offers a lesson for all women. It should be ascribed to the imaginative and artistic ingenuity of the biblical narrator that one of the most vital patriarchal concerns is repeatedly presented not as an imposition on woman but as something she herself desires more than anything else.

It must be understood that by insisting on woman's unmitigated desire for children and by making sure that the female characters

[22] Trible, *God and the Rhetoric of Sexuality*, 195–96.

[23] In his compendious and meticulous study of the origins of patriarchy, Robert Briffault points out that "the levirate custom owes its origin to the assimilation of a wife to inheritable property" (p. 776). According to Briffault, there is no real distinction between the biblical justification of the levirate as a means for "building up the brother's house" (Deut 25:5) or "raising seed unto him," and the "economic view which regards the woman as a permanent collective acquisition of the husband's group" (p. 777). Briffault traces the levirate custom "to its original source in the practice of fraternal sexual communism or polyandry" (p. 778). See *The Mothers*, Vol. I (New York: Johnson, reprinted 1927).

[24] The social plight of widows and unmarried women is well documented in the Hebrew Bible. See Phyllis Bird, "Images of Women in the Old Testament," *Religion and Sexism* (ed. Rosemary Ruether; New York: Simon & Schuster, 1974) 41–88.

dramatizing this desire are either wives or widows, the biblical narrative promotes a patriarchal ideology; it does not merely offer a psychological insight into the female nature. This becomes clear when we compare the positive mother-figures with the negative ones. The only negative characterization of mothers occurs in the story of the harlots and King Solomon. It is true that this story intends mainly to illustrate Solomon's unmatched wisdom, but at the same time it parodies the mother-figure as unmarried woman. The mother-harlot who crushes her baby son in her sleep and exchanges her dead son for her roommate's baby presents a preposterous prevarication of the standard biblical mother-figure. Her criminal neglect of her baby, her selfishness, her jealousy of the other harlot and the ruthlessness she displays toward the living baby distort the maternal attributes of love, mercy, nurturing, compassion, and tenderness. The true mother on the other hand plays the victim role. Although the text treats her less harshly, she still is far from emerging victorious, or an admirable female role model. The real hero in this story is King Solomon, whose wisdom spares the life of a male baby and restores justice to the precarious world of both females. The absence of lawful husbands from this story implies that the sordid competition over the living baby is directly related to the lack of male authority over the females and their offspring. The message seems to be that when woman gives birth outside of wedlock, there is bound to be trouble. Not only will she suffer, but her baby's life may be jeopardized. Motherhood uncontrolled by man is dangerous and sometimes fatal. King Solomon, who resolves the conflict with breathtaking brilliance, stands for the male master who alone can restore order in a world come undone by woman's unreliable nature and what appears to be her natural tendency to compete against her own sex.

It is interesting that even in this parodic scene, the biblical narrative is consistent in positing the child as woman's greatest desire; this is the most prominent character trait of the biblical mother-figure. Even a harlot's love for her child transcends her possessiveness of her children and hostility toward other women. From this point of view the mother-harlot is not very different from the respectable matriarchs, especially Rachel, whose desire for children seems to override all her other concerns. The negative and positive mother-figures share yet another common property—jealousy of and competitiveness against other mothers. The motif of motherhood in the biblical narrative seems to be closely associated with the motif of female rivalry. The mother-harlot who steals her roommate's son away and encourages the king to kill him acts on the same motivation that drove Sarah to drive out Hagar and her son Ishmael (Gen 21:9-10). Rachel too seems to be driven to despair by her jealousy of her fertile sister. The motif of female rivalry is intertwined with the motif of motherhood in the story of Hannah and Peninnah. The fertile Peninnah taunts and humiliates

Hannah for her barrenness (1 Sam 1:16). It is rare to find a biblical narrative presenting mutually supportive mothers. Again, this may reflect an authentic social situation which forced women to compete against each other in their attempt to gain the only thing that endowed them with a modicum of social respectability, namely, motherhood. But this may also be explained as a clever literary strategy in the service of biblical sexual politics. By perpetuating the theme of women's mutual rivalry, especially in a reproductive context, the narrative implies that sisterhood is a precarious alternative to the patriarchal system.

Both the positive and the negative mother-figures are shown to prefer their sons' well-being to their own. The mother-harlot is willing to give up her baby to make sure that he survives. The best consolation offered to Hagar, who has been driven out by Sarah, refers not to herself but to her son: " . . . and the angel of God called to Hagar from heaven and said to her, 'What troubles you Hagar? Fear not; for God has heard the voice of the lad where he is. Arise, lift up the lad, and hold him fast with your hand; for I will make him a great nation'" (Gen 21:17–18). This consolation, which focuses exclusively on the future son Ishmael, is presented as the only and the most effective divine response to woman's predicament. Her own physical and emotional anguish is not taken into account. The only problems biblical mothers face concern their children's well-being, and the only solution to their problems is the assurance that their children will survive. Thus the biblical narrative presents as the best palliative for a difficult pregnancy a message concerning the future children. Yahweh's promise to the pregnant Rebekah that she will bear twins seems to put an end to her intolerable pangs (Gen 25:22–24). Rachel's fatal pregnancy is presented as peripheral to the birth of Benjamin. The text that reports the midwife's consolation refers rather elliptically to the mother's fatal pain: "And when she was in her hard labor, the midwife said to her, 'Fear not; for now you will have another son'" (Gen 35:17).[25] Rachel's birth pangs are mentioned in a temporal clause, subordinated to the main clause containing the midwife's consolation. The only allusion to the mother's complaint is included in the name she gives her son, just before she dies; *"Ben-oni"* means "son of my sorrow." But even this rare and subtle allusion to woman's protest against her maternal role is subsequently deleted from the biblical record. After Rachel's death, Jacob renames his newborn son "Benjamin," which

[25] Eli's daughter-in-law also dies while giving birth and here too the Bible records the midwives' consolation rather than the mother's words: "Fear not, for you have borne a son" (1 Sam 4:20). The name that the dying mother gives her newborn baby 'î-kābôd ("no glory"), also denotes bitterness and despair, but the text interprets the name as a reflection on the national state of affairs and the loss of her husband and her father-in-law. This interpretation is ascribed to the dying woman herself and repeated twice for emphasis (1 Sam 4:21–22).

means in Hebrew "the son of my right arm." The Bible endorses the father's choice, which underscores the idea of powerfulness, in clear preference to the mother's plaintiveness.

Woman's reluctance to give birth or to assume maternal responsibility for her child is an option that is completely excluded from the represented reality of the Bible. These possibilities do not even appear as subject for criticism as they do in the case of men. Onan, for example, refuses to "raise seed unto 'his brother Er'" and consequently is severely punished by Yahweh (Gen 38:10). David, who shirks responsibility for Bathsheba's baby, is harshly rebuked by Yahweh's emissary, Nathan (2 Samuel 12). But woman is not even shown to be capable of *not* desiring children. To acknowledge woman's disinterest in children would undermine one of the major premises of patriarchal thought: that woman always desires to be a mother. The biblical narrative spares no effort in describing woman's desire for children. Rachel is described as most desperate to give birth: "Give me children, or I shall die" (Gen 30:1). Ironically, Rachel dies not through barrenness but through fertility. Rachel's despair indicates that having children is an asset that supersedes, in her eyes, her status as Jacob's preferred wife. This is emphasized in Hannah's case as well. Despite her awareness of Elkanah's love and devotion for her, Hannah is desperate and bitter over her barrenness. Deftly and effectively, the Bible presents what it values as something women themselves value most.

Mother-figures are portrayed not only as desirous of children but also as protective of their children and relentlessly devoted to them. Whereas conflicts between fathers and children appear as prevalent motifs in the biblical narrative (e.g., Laban versus Rachel and Leah; Jacob versus his sons, especially Simeon and Levi; Saul versus Jonathan and Michal; and David versus Absalom), they almost never appear in the context of mother-child relationship. The closest a mother-figure comes to being portrayed at cross-purposes with her child is Rebekah scheming against Esau, her eldest son. But Rebekah does it out of love for Jacob, rather than out of resentment for Esau.

Maternal protectiveness is normally dramatized when the child's physical survival or well-being is endangered. Examples range from Hagar and Ishmael to the Shunammite and her son. Even prostitutes are depicted as compassionate mothers, as illustrated by the real mother in the story of Solomon's trial. Perhaps the most touching image of the protective mother is embodied by Rizpah, the daughter of Aiah, who zealously guards the bodies of her dead sons from predatory animals and birds (2 Sam 21:10). Surrogate mother figures, like governesses and wet-nurses, are also portrayed primarily as protective. Mephibosheth's governess saves him from death (2 Sam 4:4), and Yehosheba, aunt and wet-nurse, saves the life of Yoash, son of Ahaziah. Only father figures are presented as capable of sacrificing the lives of their children. There is no female counterpart to

Abraham and Jephthah, except the mother who sacrifices her son to save her life (2 Kgs 6:29).

On the other hand, the "maternal instinct" is portrayed as a highly selfish and confined inclination, mostly focused on one's own child. Sarah's concern for her son Isaac is presented as her primary motivation for driving Hagar and Ishmael out (Gen 21:9–10). The harlot who lost her son shows no pity for the son of her friend and prefers to see him dead rather than alive in the arms of her rival (1 Kgs 3:26). In one of the most unnerving narratives, a mother who has agreed to kill and eat another's son during the great hunger in Samaria refuses to sacrifice her own son in her turn, as originally planned (2 Kgs 6:29).

Woman's parenthood in the biblical narrative is largely restricted to reproductive and protective functions. Hagar, Zipporah, the Shunam-mite, and Rizpah all represent the maternal role in the most rudimen-tary and, one may venture to say, simplistic forms. When a mother appears to interfere in behalf of her son in a more sophisticated way, for example, to promote his rights over his siblings she must circumvent her husband's authority. Thus, when Rebekah interferes in behalf of Jacob, she does not do so openly, for example, by attempting to convince Isaac that his preference for Esau is not in keeping with Yahweh's will. Rather, she resorts to deception, which indicates that only in this circu-itous manner will she be able to prevail over her husband. But while Rebekah takes initiative independently, Bathsheba does not dare inter-cede with David in behalf of Solomon before Nathan encourages her to do so. Here, too, mother is forced to resort to a bit of histrionics in order to win over the father, the final authority over the fate of her child. The mother may be the decisive factor in giving birth to and preserving the life of her children; but she remains subservient to her husband's author-ity over her and her children.

It is interesting to note that, whereas mothers are shown to interfere actively in behalf of their sons, they never interfere in behalf of their daughters. The story of Dinah's rape makes no reference to Leah, her mother. The only responsible parties are her father, Jacob (somewhat lamely), and her brothers. The story of Jephthah's daughter does not mention her mother either. The story of the concubine exploited to death by the Benjaminites refers to her father and her master only. Maacah, the mother of Tamar, is absent from the story about her daughter's rape. Aside from the victim, the story mentions only the aggressor, Amnon, the negligent father, David, and the avenger, Absalom, Tamar's brother. By expatiating on mothers who protect or interfere in behalf of their sons, the biblical narrative creates maternal role models which promote the interests of the male rather than the female child. In fact, the biblical narrative tends to define children in general as sons. More precisely, the children that count are all male. Thus, all the annunciation type-scenes precede the birth of sons. The biblical mothers are usually desirous of sons. This is blatant in the case of Rachel, who demands from Jacob, *hābâ lî bānîm* ("give me sons"). The English translation, rendering "sons" as "children," misses this point. The children born to previously barren mothers are all male. Similarly, Tamar and Ruth are rewarded with the birth of sons. When the biblical narrative mentions birth it almost exclusively refers to a male baby. The only exception is Dinah, Leah's daughter. But even here the daughter seems to be short-changed, since hers is the only case in which the Bible omits the etymology of the name (Gen 30:21). The motif of mother-daughter relationship is practically nonexistent in the biblical narrative. Not only is motherhood defined in relation to a lawful husband-father, but it is also determined by the male gender of the child. Furthermore, it can be asserted that the presence of mother-figures in the biblical narrative is often contingent upon the identity and importance of their sons. In other words, the narrative frequently deals with the mother-figure because of its interest in her immediate or future offspring rather than in her own character. Some narratives involving a mother-figure focus mainly on the circumstances leading to the last son's birth. Soon after the birth of the son, the mother-figure is quickly whisked off the stage (Leah, Tamar, Samson's mother, Ruth). Other mothers survive in a few details concerning their protection of their sons, for example, Sarah, Rebekah, the Shunammite and Bathsheba. Sarah manages to drive Hagar and Ishmael away (Genesis 21) shortly before she expires (Gen 23:2). Rebekah disappears from the scene as soon as her protective role is completed, allowing the literary focus to shift from Isaac to Jacob. The Shunammite disappears as soon as her son is resuscitated by Elisha, allowing the focus to shift back to Elisha. And Bathsheba disappears from the text as soon as Solomon's rule is ensured, allowing the focus to shift from David to Solomon.

The literary frame is particularly significant in the case of the annunciation type-scene, because of its unusual emphasis on the mother-figure. Even in these scenes the dramatic climax involves the birth of a son. Additionally, they all start with reference to the father. Even in the later scenes, featuring especially dominant mother-figures, the beginning deals with the father, and the ending with the son. The annunciation scene of Samson opens with an exposition relating first to Manoah and later to his wife: "And there was a certain man of Zorah, of the tribe of the Danites, whose name was Manoah; and his wife was barren and had no children" (Judg 13:2). Although Hannah clearly outshines her husband Elkanah, the annunciation type-scene opens first with reference to the man, presenting the potential mother as his barren co-wife (1 Sam 1:1–2). The Shunammite's story extols the woman's virtues, but still it constitutes only a part of a narrative series revolving around Elisha. Although she prevails over her husband in the annunciation type-scene, the narrative as a whole is presented as an additional enterprise of the man of God, another aspect of his divine power. This can be seen in the opening verses of the scene: "One day Elisha went on to Shunem, and there lived a great woman who urged (literally, seized) him to eat bread, and so whenever he passed there he would stop (literally, turn) there to eat bread" (2 Kgs 4:8). The Shunammite is introduced in a combined sentence which functions syntactically as a relative clause that refers to Shunem, the place where Elisha used to visit. This strategy is not restricted to the annunciation type-scene; it appears in the story of Tamar and Judah (Gen 38:1–5) and in the story of Ruth and Boaz (Ruth 1:1–5). Despite the unquestionably central role played by mother-figures in annunciation type-scenes and in narratives about significant births, the literary frame of the unit, opening and concluding with information regarding male characters, attests to the patriarchal ideology underlying them.

These constraints on the biblical mother-figures explain their literary flatness. None of the biblical mother-figures matches the depth and complexity of father-figures like Abraham, Jacob, Jephthah, and David. Only father figures are shown to experience conflict between, for example, parental love and the exigencies of divine authority (Abraham and Jephthah). Only they demonstrate the complexity of a situation in which a parent is called upon to scold his most beloved son, or to hide his love for fear of sibling revenge (Jacob). Only they exemplify the human conflict between love for and fear of one's own child (David). The parental role played by the father-figure constitutes only one aspect in the character, one that contributes to the depth and many-sidedness of this character. It does not eclipse his other qualities. This is the difference between a multifaceted, well-developed literary character and a type, or a role model. We must conclude that although the procreative context is the only one that allows for a direct communication between woman and Yahweh (or his messenger), and although motherhood is the most exalted female role in the biblical narrative, the biblical mother-figures attain neither the human nor the literary complexity of their male counterparts. The patriarchal framework of the biblical story prevents the mother-figure from becoming a full-fledged *human* role model, while its androcentric perspective confines her to a limited literary role, largely subordinated to the biblical male protagonists.

8

WHO IS HIDING THE TRUTH?
DECEPTIVE WOMEN AND BIBLICAL ANDROCENTRISM

Esther Fuchs

Deceptiveness is a common characteristic of women in the Hebrew Bible. It is a motif that runs through most narratives involving women, both condemnatory and laudatory ones. From Eve to Esther, from Rebekah to Ruth, the characterization of women presents deceptiveness as an almost inescapable feature of femininity. The message that such characterizations convey is explicit in Ecclesiastes: "And I found more bitter than death the woman whose heart is snares and nets, and whose hands are fetters; he who pleases God escapes her but the sinner is taken by her" (Eccl 7:26).[1] In this exploratory essay, I would like to examine the close association of woman and deceptiveness in the context of power-structured relations between men and women in the Hebrew Bible. My main focus will be on the manner in which the biblical narrative uses literary strategies in order to foster and perpetuate its patriarchal ideology. This essay suggests that the presentation of women as characters who hide the truth reveals not only the extent of the Bible's androcentric bias but also the manner in which the biblical narrative suppresses the truth about woman's subjugation within the patriarchal framework.

One of the things that the biblical text fails to make explicit in its treatment of deceptive acts perpetrated by women is their close relationship to woman's inferior social position and political powerlessness in patriarchal society. Rebekah's deception of the old and blind Isaac does not so much as hint at the wife's powerlessness versus her husband. It does not take into account that deception is Rebekah's only means of granting her preferred son a blessing. The fact is that Isaac, despite his dramatized impotence, is superior to Rebekah in power, yet it is Rebekah who is presented as a powerful woman who outsmarts an ailing old man.[2]

---

[1] This and all the following quotations are based on the RSV (1952) unless otherwise indicated.

[2] For a feminist rehabilitation of Rebekah see Christine Garside Allen, "Who Was Rebekah? 'On Me Be the Curse, My Son,'" *Beyond Androcentrism—New Essays on*

In the first place it is Rebekah who initiates the act of deception (Gen 27:5–6). Eavesdropping on Isaac's conversation with Esau, in which the father asks his son to bring him game and savory food before he gives him his blessing, Rebekah summons Jacob and *orders* him to follow her scheme: "Now therefore, my son, obey my word as I command you. Go to the flock and fetch me two good kids, that I may prepare from them savory food for your father, such as he loves; and you shall bring it to your father to eat, so that he may bless you before he dies" (Gen 27:8–10). When Jacob protests that Isaac will surely recognize him for he is "a smooth" man, whereas Esau is "hairy," Rebekah remains undaunted: "Upon me be the curse, my son; only obey my word, and go fetch them to me" (v 13). The detailed description of the deception revolves around Rebekah, while Jacob plays the role of the obedient son. The text does not condemn Rebekah for her deceptiveness. On the contrary, it implies that her actions are in harmony with Yahweh's plan. But if Rebekah acts in accordance with Yahweh's will, why does she resort to deception? The fact is that Rebekah deceives Isaac not because she is a devious wife but because legally she is inferior and subordinate to Isaac. Within biblical patriarchy, the institute of primogeniture and parental blessings applied strictly to males. Mothers could not give blessings to their children any more than daughters could receive them. Had Rebekah been able to express her love for Jacob through maternal blessings, she would not have needed to use deception. She would have in all probability blessed Jacob by herself. Although the narrative presents the woman as a strong-willed character, who outsmarts her husband and acts out her wishes, Rebekah is in fact as underprivileged as her son Jacob. Had Rebekah been socially and legally equal to her husband, deception would have been unnecessary.

Potiphar's wife is another female character presented as an insidious and powerful wife. Rejected by her handsome Hebrew servant Joseph, the exasperated Egyptian court lady decides to win him by force: "she caught him by his garment, saying: 'Lie with me'" (Gen 39:12). The faithful Joseph refuses to betray his master and flees, leaving his garment in the woman's hands. The deceitful woman turns the symbol of Joseph's innocence into incriminating evidence: "The Hebrew servant whom you have brought among us, came into me to insult me; but as soon as I lifted up my voice and cried, he left his garment with me, and fled out of the house" (Gen 39:17–18). Although the narrative does not condemn Potiphar's wife directly, it does so implicitly through the detailed description of her deceptive histrionics. What the narrative does *not*

Women and Religion (ed. Rita M. Gross; Missoula, MT: Scholars Press, 1977) 183–216. Allen takes the view that Rebekah was grossly misjudged by biblical interpreters rather than by the text itself.

consider is the double standard it uses in its condemnation of Potiphar's wife. Had Potiphar himself seduced a maid servant he would not have been condemned for either betraying or deceiving his wife, since patriarchal monogamy applies exclusively to women.[3] Since the wife's legal status vis-à-vis her husband was little more than that of a servant, only she stood to be condemned for her betrayal of her husband-master. It is doubtful that the biblical narrative would have found it necessary to report an incident in which the husband deceives his wife having seduced one of his maid servants, let alone condemn him for it.

Having considered the deceptive woman as mother and wife, it is now time to turn to the deceptive daughter in the biblical narrative. One of the most prominent examples in this regard is Rachel. The Bible tells us that Rachel steals her father's idols (tĕrāpîm) without explaining her motives (Gen 31:19). As much as the narrative derides the treacherous Laban and his idol worship, the validity of Rachel's actions remains highly questionable, especially when contrasted with Jacob's uprightness. Despite his continuous exploitation by Laban, Jacob departs from his father-in-law's house taking only what legally belongs to him. One wonders, however, if Rachel would have to deceive her father were she entitled to his inheritance as a son would be.[4] Since daughters are not allowed to share their father's inheritance, the only way in which Rachel could appropriate any of her father's possessions was through theft. As she and Leah put it themselves: "Is there any portion or inheritance left to us in our father's house?" (Gen 31:14). While the text describes in detail Rachel's devious trick, sitting atop the camel on the stolen gods and claiming that she cannot get up because "the way of women is upon" her (31:35), it remains silent about her motivation. It is of course possible that Rachel steals her father's gods out of spite or vindictiveness, a motivation well justified considering her father's treatment of her; nevertheless, this justification would not have counterbalanced—even if it were explicitly stated in the text—the negative implications generated by her presentation as a deceptive daughter.

The histrionic device used by Achsah, the daughter of Caleb, in order to win fertile land from her father is another episode presenting the deceptive daughter in a highly ambiguous light. In all likelihood Achsah would not have had to use pretense in her attempt to secure property for herself had she not been a woman (Josh 15:18). Achsah, who was "given" by Caleb, her father, as prize to Othniel (Josh 15:17) for conquering Kiriath-sepher, is

---

[3] On the position of wives in biblical patriarchy, see Roland de Vaux, *Ancient Israel* (New York and Toronto: McGraw-Hill, reprinted 1965) 1. 24–40. See also Phyllis Bird, "Images of Women in the Old Testament," *Religion and Sexism* (ed. Rosemary R. Ruether; New York: Simon and Schuster, 1974) 41–88.

[4] *Ancient Israel*, 1. 24–26.

compelled deceptively to coax her father into giving her what a son would have obtained by right.[5]

Even when women's motivation for deceiving is defensible, their very act of deception produces an ambivalent effect that is bound to compromise their character as a whole. Lot's daughters deceptively inebriate and have illicit intercourse with their father for a good reason, to continue the human race (Gen 19:31–32). Yet, the deceptive means by which they seek to fulfill their goal casts a questionable light on their conduct. The final evaluation of their conduct is implied by the fact that their sons become Israel's archenemies: Ammon and Moab. In the final analysis Lot's daughters act in accordance with their foremost duty within the framework of biblical patriarchy. Had they been male, they may have been able to act with the magnanimity of Shem and Japheth, who respectfully cover their naked father, Noah, as he lies drunk in his tent, rather than exploit his nakedness (Gen 9:23).

To challenge the authority of her father the biblical daughter almost invariably resorts to deception. Sons, on the other hand, use direct means as well. Jonathan challenges his father Saul on behalf of David, whereas Michal, in order to save David's life, uses deception (1 Sam 19:12–17).

In most cases woman's deception of man is motivated by fear and impotence, but the biblical text rarely refers to this factor. In contrast, it is careful to point out fear when it serves as the motivating principle behind man's deception of man. Thus the Bible stresses that Abram deceives Pharaoh concerning the true identity of Sarai, his wife, out of fear for his life. Recognizing his inferior political status as Pharaoh's subject, Abram urges his wife to collaborate with him: "Say you are my sister, that it may go well with me because of you, and that my life be spared on your account" (Gen 12:13). Isaac too pretends that Rebekah is his sister "for he feared to say 'my wife'" (Gen 26:7). Woman's fear of man, on the other hand, is not made explicit as her motive for deception.

The biblical text ignores the factor of woman's subordination to man underlying her nefarious behavior pattern. Instead of pointing up the inevitable link between her alleged deceptiveness and her powerlessness, the biblical text dramatizes her deceptiveness as her most lethal and effective weapon against man. The deceptive woman is normally condemned when she wields deception to gain something for herself. Delilah, for example, deceives Samson in exchange for money: "And the lords of the Philistines came to her and said to her: 'Entice him and see wherein his great strength lies, and by what means we may overpower him, that we may bind him to subdue him; and we will each give you eleven hundred pieces of silver'" (Judg 16:5). The characterization of Delilah reflects the Israelite fear and distrust of the foreign woman. Delilah's successful

5 *Ancient Israel*, 1. 53–55.

deception of Samson spells a lesson in national as well as in sexual politics; do not trust women, especially if they happen to be foreign and beautiful. Jezebel is not only a foreign woman but also a powerful queen. As such she presents a threatening image in the biblical frame of reference. The Bible imputes to Jezebel as well an act of deception. She is said to have staged a false trial against Naboth the Jezreelite for refusing to sell his vineyard to Ahab, the king (1 Kgs 21:8–11). For her deceptiveness and her idolatrous transgressions Jezebel is brutally penalized: "So they threw her down; and some of her blood spattered on the wall and on the horses and they trampled on her" (2 Kgs 9:33).

The biblical double standard becomes clear when we compare Jezebel's deception of Naboth with King David's deception of Uriah. Not only does David deceive an innocent man, he deceives one of his most loyal and dedicated subjects (2 Samuel 11). Both rulers covet a possession that does not belong to them. In the case of Jezebel it is Naboth's vineyard, in the case of David it is Bathsheba, Uriah's wife. Jezebel accuses Naboth falsely and brings about his death, while David orders Uriah dead in order to appropriate to himself the Hittite's wife. Yet David is given a chance to repent, be punished, and finally be absolved. Not only is he forgiven for his deception, murder, and unlawful appropriation of another's property, but he is allowed to keep this property and make her into a wife. Jezebel is not given a similar chance.

Deception in male-related contexts is condoned, even recommended when the underprivileged deceiver struggles for dominance over his superior or oppressor. Women's deception on the other hand is condemned when it appears to be self-serving. Women retain a semblance of respectability when their deception assists a weaker male in a power struggle against a stronger one. (Incidents depicting women deceiving men for the sake of another woman are non-existent in the Bible). When Rachel deceives Laban, she sides with her exploited husband, Jacob. Michal deceives Saul for the sake of the persecuted David, and Rebekah deceives Isaac for the sake of Jacob.

On the national level, women assisting the Israelites against their usually mightier enemies are exonerated and even extolled. Thus Rahab, who deceives her own people and assists the Israelite spies, is a positive role model (Joshua 2). Similarly Jael the Midianite, who deceptively kills Sisera the Canaanite, is praised for her valor and cunning: "Most blessed of women be Jael, the wife of Heber the Kenite, of tent-dwelling women most blessed. He asked water and she gave him milk, she brought him curds in a lordly bowl. She put her hand to the tent peg and her right hand to the workmen's mallet; she struck Sisera a blow, she crushed his head, she shattered and pierced his temple" (Judg 5:24–26).

Solidarity with one's late husband is another factor that commonly rewards woman for her deceptive acts. Examples are Tamar and Ruth, who deceive in order to insure the patrilineage of their late husbands. Tamar dresses up as a prostitute and seduces Judah, her father-in-law. When discovered pregnant, Tamar is ordered by Judah to be put to death (Gen 38:24). This indicates the risk Tamar takes in her efffort to perpetuate the name of Er. The paradox is that Tamar deceives Judah for his own sake. For her self-abnegation and loyalty to her husband, Tamar is rewarded by giving birth to Perez, King David's progenitor. Tamar's deceptiveness is construed as a heroic deed, not as a product of female guile. In the final analysis Tamar is exalted for her acceptance of the patriarchal status quo. Instead of protesting the unjust lot of a widow bound to remain unmarried, Tamar endorses these constraints and even uses deceit to ensure their perpetuation.

Ruth is yet another heroine who uses deception, although in a milder form, in order to marry Boaz, a relative of her late husband Mahlon. Rather than approach Boaz directly, Ruth first disguises her own identity and, only in the middle of the night when he wakes up startled to find her sleeping by his feet in the barn, reveals her identity and asks for his protection (i.e., marriage) (Ruth 3:9). Ruth's cunning initiative and loyalty to Mahlon reward her with giving birth to Obed, the grandfather of King David (Ruth 4:21–22).

Woman's deception is acceptable and even recommended when her motives are selfless and when she attempts to promote the cause of man. Yet the ascription of deceptiveness even to the most exalted female role models tarnishes their luminousness. Rebekah's support of Jacob is in compliance with Yahweh's preference, but the detailed dramatization of her unscrupulous deception of her helpless husband and unsuspecting son detracts from her moral stature and imprints her with an indelible culpability. Jael's courageous loyalty to the Israelites is indeed highly praised in the biblical text, but the repeated dramatization of the deceptively hospitable welcome she extends to the exhausted Sisera injects her image with a foul taste of treachery. It is true that she is extolled as a national heroine, but she also emerges as a threatening figure in the context of relations between men and women. If the negative characterization of foreign powerful women conveys a clear didactic message to the male reader, the positive characterization of treacherous women conveys an ambivalent message concerning the female "race." The safest thing for man to do is to distrust woman, or as the book of Ecclesiastes put it: ". . . he who pleases God escapes her" (Eccl 7:26).

The discriminatory treatment of deceptive women is reflected in two major strategies manipulated by the biblical text: the suppression of motivation, especially when the deceptive act is directly related to woman's inferior status and political powerlessness, and the negative presentation of women who deceive for causes that are not meant to enhance male power.

This discriminatory treatment produces female portraits intended, among other things, to validate the suspicion that women's apparent impotence is nothing but a deceptive disguise, that underneath their vulnerable coyness lurks a dangerously calculating mind. This suspicion is dramatized in "positive" role models, such as Jael or Rahab, as much as in negative ones, such as Delilah and Jezebel. It underlies the characterization of the biblical matriarchs as much as it does the nameless harlot in Solomon's trial. To the extent that female biblical characters are fictional, the repeated ascription of deceptiveness to them reveals not only a distrusting gynophobia but also a political statement that seeks to perpetuate the subordination of women based on their alleged moral deficiency. The character of Eve is a case in point. The narrative ignores the fact that having been created from and for Adam (according to Genesis 2), Eve is already a priori subordinate to him. It also disregards the possible link between this state of subordination and her susceptibility to the serpent's words; having missed the direct instructions of God, which could possibly counteract her impressionability, Eve receives the divine injunction through the mediation of Adam. For her deceptiveness and disobedience, which could be linked to her a priori subordination, she is penalized with a greater degree of subordination to her husband (Gen 3:16). By ascribing moral inferiority to the first woman, the story of Genesis seeks to justify her social inferiority and to promote the ideology that supports man's supremacy over woman.

The strategic manipulation of narrative for ideological purposes is not different essentially in narrative contexts that may conceivably represent historical events and characters. By allowing women only a secondary literary status, the biblical narrative foregrounds woman's deceptiveness to a far greater extent than it does in the case of male biblical heroes. Thus Rahab, Jael, Delilah, and Jezebel are characterized mostly through the dramatization of their deceptive acts, whether positively or negatively evaluated. Rachel's and Rebekah's deceptive acts are also far more emphasized than, for example, the deceptive acts of Abraham, Jacob, or David, if only by the mere fact that as secondary characters they are not allowed to evolve and change. The scenic dramatization of women's virtue is not detailed enough to counterbalance the impact of their deceptiveness, and, very often, their virtuous and deceptive acts are inextricably intertwined in a single scene that speaks for their entire character.

Celebrated or denigrated, the characters of deceptive women, which constitute the majority of female characters in the Bible, serve as an effective ideological tool that perpetuates the suspicion and distrust of women, and that validates women's subordination through discriminatory literary techniques. Our awareness of the double standard underlying both their presentation and their evaluation helps us realize that the recurrent association of femaleness and deceptiveness reflects a gyno-phobic and patriarchal attitude rather than an inherent moral deficiency that predisposes women to dishonesty. The alleged female deceptiveness is not a product of woman's innate insidiousness but a result of the power-structured relations between men and women as reflected in the artistic construction of the biblical narrative. The real deception is not committed by biblical women but by the androcentric text, which ignores or suppresses the motivations of the female character, especially when they are related to her powerlessness vis-à-vis men, and which applies discriminating evaluative bench marks to her conduct. The biblical text ignores the fact that if indeed prevalent, female deception of men stems from women's subordinate social status and from the fact that patriarchy debars them from direct action. By uncovering this hidden fact we may be in a better position to understand and reevaluate what appears to be one of the most ambiguous characteristics of women in the Hebrew Bible.